THE STORIES OF WOMEN

Meet Me in the Bible Studies

Colossians and Philemon

The Stories of Women

The Story of Abraham

The Story of Jacob

"Simple and straightforward, Meet Me in the Bible is a wonderful resource to gain foundational skills in studying the Bible. If you want to feel confident in mining Scripture for God's truths and applying it to your life, this is an incredible guide."

Laura Wifler, Cofounder, Risen Motherhood; coauthor, *Risen Motherhood: Gospel Hope for Everyday Moments*

"I was greeted by the bright smile of Colleen Searcy over thirty years ago when I walked into a youth group in West Texas as a freckle-faced, curly headed, unbelieving teenager. Over the last three decades, I have watched Colleen cling to God's word, teach God's word, sing God's word, and live God's word. If you are looking to *meet* God in the Scriptures, I can think of no better guide than my friend Colleen. She will help you taste and see that the Lord is good!"

Shane Barnard, singer-songwriter, Shane and Shane

"Colleen Searcy is one of my favorite Bible teachers. You will sense her open-armed ministry within the framework of her Meet Me in the Bible series, in which she's thoughtfully prepared a table for women to feast on God's word. Whether you are an individual hungry to know God more, a small group desiring an accessible way to study together, or a women's ministry leader looking for a foundational resource for your teaching team, the Meet Me in the Bible series is a trustworthy guide."

Caroline Saunders, author, *Come Home: Tracing God's Promise of Home through Scripture*

"I've benefited from Colleen's wisdom, teaching, and partnership in ministry for a number of years. She is a gifted Bible teacher who uses her skills to invite others into biblical literacy. In the Meet Me in the Bible series, she provides what few studies do—an opportunity for women to gather for both in person teaching and discussion. You will be equipped to not only study for yourself but also cultivate teaching gifts in the lives of the women in your church. I can't wait to recommend this to my ministry friends."

Courtney Reissig, author, *Teach Me to Feel: Worshiping through the Psalms in Every Season of Life*

"As the CEO of a worldwide mission agency, I highly recommend Colleen Searcy's Meet Me in the Bible series for anyone interested in going deeper in their study of the Bible. Colleen uses a structured approach with guiding prompts that are fully interactive and enhance your reflection on Scripture. These books are helpful resources for pursuing individual study or leading a Bible study group, and these studies are culturally relevant for all groups of people. Meet Me in the Bible is an excellent and well-rounded framework that can make studying the Bible a more engaging and enriching experience for anyone."

Kurt Nelson, CEO, East-West Ministries

"I have seen firsthand the fruit of Meet Me in the Bible. Colleen's accessible framework for studying the Scripture has had a large and lasting impact on our church. Many in our congregation are still reaping the benefits of her investment in our women's ministry. If you are a seasoned student of the Scripture or are just getting started, Meet Me in the Bible will launch you into a greater exploration of the Bible and a deeper enjoyment of the God it reveals."

JR Vassar, Lead Pastor, Church at the Cross, Grapevine, Texas; author, *Glory Hunger*

MEET ME IN THE BIBLE

THE STORIES OF WOMEN

AN 8-WEEK BIBLE STUDY

COLLEEN D. SEARCY

Foreword by Jen Wilkin

WHEATON, ILLINOIS

The Stories of Women: An 8-Week Bible Study

Published by Crossway
1300 Crescent Street
Wheaton, Illinois 60187

Tool 1, "Bible Timeline," designed by Brooke Hawkins.

Cover illustration and design by Brooke Hawkins
First printing 2025
Printed in China

Trade paperback ISBN: 978-1-4335-9681-0
ePub ISBN: 978-1-4335-9683-4
PDF ISBN: 978-1-4335-9682-7

Crossway is a publishing ministry of Good News Publishers.

RRD 34 33 32 31 30 29 28 27 26 25
15 14 13 12 11 10 9 8 7 6 5 4 3 2

CONTENTS

FOREWORD

For the past twenty-five years, my primary place of ministry has been the local church, and my primary aim has been to build Bible literacy among women. So, naturally, any time I'm asked to endorse a resource, I ask myself how it will serve that context. That's why I'm particularly excited to bring to your attention the Meet Me in the Bible series.

When evaluating a resource, I hold two important questions in view: (1) Is this from a trustworthy voice? and (2) Does this challenge those who use it to grow in their ability to read and understand the Scriptures? I want to help answer both of those questions for you as you consider how the Meet Me in the Bible series might help you personally, or those you serve in your church.

In terms of the trustworthiness of the author, I can speak with confidence that Colleen Searcy is an excellent guide. I first met Colleen in 2008, about a year after moving to Dallas and joining a new church. I was looking for other women in the church who shared my desire to see women equipped with solid discipleship opportunities. Colleen and I went to coffee, and I knew I had found a like-minded partner. Since that time, we have together taught, written curriculum, led teams, and prayed—all from that desire to see God's daughters grounded in the Scriptures. Colleen is not only theologically and biblically solid; she is a gifted teacher, humble and kind, and a faithful friend.

In terms of the usefulness of the resource, Meet Me in the Bible so closely aligns with my own philosophy of teaching that I can recommend it eagerly. It's a brilliant combination of a Scripture journal and a guide for growing in Bible literacy. It encourages the user to practice the time-tested method of "observe, interpret, apply" in a way that allows understanding to grow gradually. It presses us to be active learners rather than passive consumers, not rushing to commentaries, but sitting with the text, patiently waiting for our own understanding to begin to emerge. For those who know my method and Bible studies, Meet Me in the Bible will feel familiar in the best ways.

It is a streamlined approach suitable for personal study as well as an excellent foundation for group discussion and teaching environments.

The skills taught in each Meet Me in the Bible study will help you understand a particular book of the Bible better. But they will also help you understand *any* book (or books) of the Bible better as you grow in your ability to use those skills. And because application focuses on relationship—with God, self, and others—these skills will help you to live and love like a Christ follower.

So it is my pleasure to commend to you both a trusted guide and a trustworthy resource. My guess is that if you had come to coffee with Colleen and me on that day some years ago, you would have shared our excitement to see women growing in their love of the Scriptures and of the God they proclaim. What we want for you is to be able to serve your local church, whether in a classroom or a living room, with good tools and the confidence to use them. My prayer is that you would take what Colleen has created and combine it with an invitation to the women God has placed in your sphere of influence—a simple invitation: Meet me in the Bible! No sweeter fellowship is found than in that meeting place. May your time spent there yield the richest of treasures.

JEN WILKIN
Bible teacher; author, *Women of the Word*;
None Like Him; and *In His Image*

MEET ME IN THE BIBLE

A Simple Framework for Reading the Bible and Enjoying God

God delights in revealing himself, and one of the primary ways he reveals himself is through the Bible. My deep desire is for people to know and enjoy God through the study of his word. I want people with all kinds of personalities and learning styles to grow in confidence that they can read and study their Bibles. This framework of Bible study was designed to provide helpful structure and a lot of freedom for the studier.

The *Why* behind Meet Me in the Bible

Meet Me in the Bible is a simple, five-step framework designed to help you read your Bible. It is not a fill-in-the-blank study. After numerous conversations with women over many years of ministry, I've found that countless women do Bible studies, yet few feel confident opening the Bible and reading it on their own. And although many women desire to lead a Bible study, few feel equipped to do so. Meet Me in the Bible offers a method to help you do both.

How to Use Meet Me in the Bible

This framework was designed for either individual or group Bible study, and it incorporates the time-tested stages of Bible reading: observation, interpretation, and application. Prompts are provided on your bookmark to help you observe, interpret, and apply the Scriptures. You will also be prompted to use simple and accessible tools as you study. You will grow in confidence and find your pace as you practice observing, interpreting, and applying the Scriptures again and again. You can use this framework to study any book of the Bible.

For Group Study

If you are doing this study as part of a group, you will want to complete each lesson before you meet. Each lesson is divided into five doable steps rather than five assigned days, to allow flexibility. You can work through one step each day or the whole lesson in one sitting. Find the pace that works best for you. No matter how much of the lesson you are able to complete, please don't skip gathering with your Bible study group. You will benefit from your group, and your group will be encouraged by your presence.

Meet Me in the Bible studies are meant to be flexible. Group studies can opt to meet in small groups for discussion and a time of teaching or simply meet for discussion only.

TIPS FOR GROUPS THAT OPT TO MEET FOR BOTH A TIME OF DISCUSSION AND A TIME OF TEACHING

- If this is your group's first Meet Me in the Bible study, be sure each participant is familiar with how to use the Meet Me in the Bible framework before you meet. You can find my videos on how to use the Meet Me in the Bible framework at colleensearcy.com /mmibteaching. In these videos, I demonstrate how to cross-reference, quickly check other translations, and more, using simple and free digital tools.

- For the first meeting, teachers will want to cover the Getting Started section before discussion. One of the greatest Bible study tools available is the historical context of the Bible book you are studying. To have the best chance of interpreting the Scriptures correctly, you need to know who the author was, whom he was writing to, the literary style he used, and what was happening in the world when he wrote it. I cover the answers to these questions in my "Getting Started" video, which you will find at colleensearcy.com /mmibteaching.

- After answering those preliminary questions, move to small-group discussion. Spend time getting to know one another. You can use the Getting Started questions in Tool 7 of the Tool Kit.

- For all future meetings, you can gather for discussion before or after the teaching. I suggest that you gather *before* the teaching. You will be amazed at the insights gained as each participant shares what was discovered during personal study. Confidence will grow as you learn from one another's discoveries. Tips for discussion:

  - The prompts on your bookmark make good points of discussion. (What did you learn from the repeated words? What was hard to understand? What did you learn about people?)
  - Content-specific discussion questions for each lesson can be found in Tool 7 of the Tool Kit.
  - Additional historical context is given in the questions in Tool 7 of the Tool Kit.
  - The bounce questions in Tool 7 of the Tool Kit are intended to jumpstart discussion and provide an easy transition to the content.
  - Discussion leaders may use as many or as few discussion questions from Tool 7 as they'd like. These questions were written to help you think deeply about the text. Many of the questions do not have one right answer and are meant to encourage further thought and robust discussion. Questions with one correct answer (e.g., What did Paul say about sin in verse 12?) can feel like a quiz rather than an invitation into conversation.

- Discussion leaders *do* want to plan which questions they will cover and think through their own answers before the group meets. They *do not* need to feel pressure to answer every question that surfaces during Bible study. The purpose of Bible study is not to impress with our knowledge; it is to grow in our knowledge of and love for God as we get to know him better through the study of his word. Enjoy being a colearner with those you are studying alongside. If the questions that surface are not answered in the teaching time, you can circle back with your group after you've had time to think further about them.

- Use the prayer pages in Tool 6 of the Tool Kit to record personal prayer requests and the prayers of those you are studying alongside.

TIPS FOR GROUPS THAT OPT TO MEET FOR DISCUSSION ONLY

- If this is your group's first Meet Me in the Bible study, be sure each participant watches my videos on how to use the Meet Me in the Bible framework before you meet. You can find them at colleensearcy.com/mmibteaching. In these videos, I demonstrate how to cross-reference, quickly check other translations, and more, using simple and free digital tools.

- For the first meeting, be prepared to discuss the Getting Started section. One of the greatest Bible study tools available is the historical context of the Bible book you are studying. To have the best chance of interpreting the Scriptures correctly, you need to know who the author was, whom he was writing to, the literary style he used, and what was happening in the world when he wrote it. I answer these questions in my "Getting Started" video at colleensearcy.com/mmibteaching.

- Spend time getting to know one another. You can use the Getting Started questions in Tool 7 of the Tool Kit.

- For all future meetings:

    - The prompts on your bookmark make good points of discussion: What did you learn from the repeated words? What was hard to understand? What did you learn about people?

    - Content-specific discussion questions for each lesson can be found in Tool 7 of the Tool Kit.

    - The bounce questions in Tool 7 of the Tool Kit are intended to jumpstart discussion and provide an easy transition to the content.

    - Additional historical context is given in the questions found in Tool 7 of the Tool Kit.

    - Discussion leaders may use as many or as few discussion questions from Tool 7 as they'd like. These questions were written to help you think deeply about the text. Many of the questions do not have one right answer and are meant to encourage further thought and robust discussion. Questions with one correct answer (e.g., What did Paul say about sin in verse 12?) can feel like a quiz rather than an invitation into conversation.

- Discussion leaders *do* want to plan on which questions they will cover and think through their own answers before the group meets. They *do not* need to feel pressure to answer every question that surfaces during Bible study. The purpose of Bible study is not to impress with our knowledge; it is to grow in our knowledge of and love for God as we get to know him better through the study of his word. When stumped by a question, you can say something like, "That is a great question! I'd like to give that more thought and circle back next time we meet." Then have fun studying! Enjoy being a colearner with those you are studying alongside. Ask God to help you with the questions that surface. He is delighted to meet you in the Bible. What a great discussion you will have the next time you meet!

- Use the prayer pages in Tool 6 of the Tool Kit to record personal prayer requests and the prayers of those you are studying alongside.

For Individual Study

- If you are doing this study on your own, you will want to begin by watching my videos on how to use the Meet Me in the Bible framework. You can find them at colleensearcy.com/mmibteaching. In these videos, I demonstrate how to cross-reference, quickly check other translations, and more, using simple and free digital tools.

- Be sure to complete the Getting Started section before diving in to study the passages of Scripture. One of the greatest Bible study tools available is the historical context of the Bible book you are studying. When you study a passage that is hard to understand, overlay the passage with the context. To have the best chance of interpreting the Scriptures correctly, we need to know who the author was, whom he was writing to, the literary style he used, and what was happening in the world when he wrote it. I answer these questions in my "Getting Started" video at colleensearcy.com/mmibteaching.

- After completing the Getting Started section, each lesson is divided into five doable steps rather than five assigned days, to allow flexibility. You can work through one step each day or work through the whole lesson in one sitting. Find the pace that works best for you.

- For a deeper dive, use the questions in Tool 7 of the Tool Kit. Additional historical context is also given within the questions. These questions were written to help you think deeply about the text.

- Use the prayer pages in Tool 6 of the Tool Kit to record your prayers while you study.

What's Included in This Study

Bible Study Bookmark

All Meet Me in the Bible studies include a bookmark with the time-tested stages of Bible reading (Observe, Interpret, and Apply) on the front. You will see the five-step framework for reading the Bible on the back of the bookmark, including prompts to help you observe, interpret, and apply the Scriptures. You will also be prompted to pause in your study to listen to and enjoy God. He wants to meet you in your study of the Bible! Although the Bible study bookmark and the Bible study book were designed to work together, your bookmark can also be used alone. It was designed to help you study any book of the Bible, and my hope is that you will use your bookmark again and again.

Bible Study Book

The book includes word-for-word Bible text. Mark it up! If you love highlighters, highlight away! If you prefer to draw symbols, grab colored pencils and go for it. Or simply underline with your favorite pen. Your Bible study book also includes titles and designated spaces that correspond with the titles and prompts on your bookmark. Additionally, you will find blank note pages throughout your book to use as you wish. Draw a chart, sketch an image, or write the lyrics to a song. Each lesson concludes with an important wrap-up question to prompt you to consider what you discovered in the Scriptures.

Meet Me in the Bible Tool Kit

Tool 1: *Bible Timeline.* Understanding historical context is key to reading and interpreting the Scriptures. Place an *X* on the simple timeline of the Bible to indicate where the scriptures you are studying land in the whole story of the Bible.

Tool 2: *Map.* Referencing a map while studying is a helpful reminder that these are stories of real people in real places.

Tool 3: *Bible Genres.* Knowing the literary style of the book of the Bible you are studying is key to correct interpretation. Just as you would approach the poems of Wordsworth differently than you would approach a history book about World War II, there are nuances to different literary styles in the Bible that must be kept in mind while interpreting and applying the Scriptures. Use this resource to identify the literary style of the book you are studying.

Tool 4: *Attributes of God.* You will be prompted to use this tool each week. You may want to mark it with a paper clip so you can turn there easily. The ultimate goal of Bible study is to know and love God, and my prayer is that your hope will be further anchored in him as you are reminded of his attributes.

Tool 5: *Bookmark Content.* All the information on your bookmark is included here for your convenience.

Tool 6: *Prayer Pages.* Use these pages to record personal prayers and prayer requests of those studying alongside you.

Tool 7: *Questions for Further Thought and Discussion*. Use as many or as few of these questions as you'd like in your individual or group study. Additional historical context is included in the questions. The bounce questions are intended to jumpstart discussion and provide an easy transition to the content. The remaining questions were written to help you think deeply about the text.

Additional Tools for Your Study

1. *Different Bible translations*. Reading Scripture verses in different Bible translations can give helpful insight as you study. This book includes the ESV translation. Other translations I recommend are the New International Version (NIV), the New Living Translation (NLT), the Christian Standard Bible (CSB), and the New American Standard Bible (NASB). I use The Message as a commentary when I study.

2. *Dictionary and thesaurus*. Look up unfamiliar words as well as "church" words such as *atonement, propitiation,* and *covenant*. You will be surprised how much clarity can be gained by reading simple definitions and synonyms in a dictionary or thesaurus.[1]

3. *Cross-references*. Cross-references are included in study Bibles, usually in the middle or at the bottom of a page. A cross-reference is a marker in the Bible pointing to other passages of Scripture with related words and themes. It is usually designated with a superscript (tiny, raised) letter. Cross-referencing is a way to use Scripture to rightly interpret Scripture. You can also use digital tools to cross-reference.[2]

4. *Study Bible footnotes*. If you have a study Bible, the provided footnotes give helpful insights.[3] Wait to check footnotes until after you've observed the text and attempted interpretation using other translations, a dictionary, and cross-references, and overlaying the passage with the context. Resist the temptation to jump to someone else's thoughts before observing and interpreting on your own. Enjoy being curious and see what you discover!

5. *Commentaries.* Commentaries can be helpful in Bible study, but wait to use commentaries until after you've observed the text and attempted interpretation using other translations, a dictionary, and cross-references, and overlaying the passage with the context. Ask God for insight as you study, and be willing to wait to hear from him. Again, resist the temptation to jump to someone else's thoughts before observing and interpreting on your own. For help choosing commentaries, begin by asking trusted leaders about their favorites.[4]

The ultimate goal of Bible study is to know and love God. So observe, interpret, apply, and enjoy God! Stay in conversation with him, asking him to help you understand the Scriptures. Ask him your hard questions. Listen to him. He wants to meet you in your study of the Bible!

WHY STUDY THE STORIES OF WOMEN?

With all the curiosity and discussion around the roles of women, it is important to search the Scriptures for answers.

The Scriptures reveal what God is like:

- He is creative. He made all things, from the blue of the sky to the planet Jupiter.
- He is a compassionate parent and will fiercely protect those he loves.
- He is deeply relational and attentive to the needs of people.
- He is on mission to save, not wishing that any should perish.
- He is gentle, and he is intense.

Women were made in God's likeness (Gen. 1:27):

- Women image God in their creativity, from writing songs to designing spreadsheets.
- Women are compassionate and will fiercely protect those they love.
- Like their Creator, women are deeply relational and attentive to the needs of people.
- Women are on mission in other countries, in office buildings, in their homes, and through prayer.
- Women image God in their gentleness and in their intensity.

Throughout the Bible, we see God engage with and invite all kinds of women to image him in different ways—single and married, young and old, different ethnicities, homemakers and warriors. Why did I choose these particular stories of women?

- It was important to me to include single and married women.
- I chose stories that include enough text to encourage line-by-line inductive study, which is the preferred method of Meet Me in the Bible studies.
- I chose stories with interesting relationships between women, such as mother and daughter, sisters, cousins, and colaborers for the kingdom of God.

Keep in mind that all the stories in this study were written as historical narratives. The authors of history books recorded the facts about what happened rather than what *should* have happened had people obeyed God. The authors did not record how they felt about what happened. This is important to keep in mind while studying stories like Sarah and Hagar and Leah and Rachel. For example, the author of Genesis recorded that Jacob chose to marry Rachel after he was married to Leah. This is what happened, but it does not mean that polygamy was acceptable to God (Gen. 2:24).

This study is about women, but it is ultimately about the God who created women, giving them blessing, dominion, dignity, and purpose (Gen. 1:26–31). My hope is that you will get to know God better and better through these stories! He delights to meet you in your study of the Bible.

Joyfully,
COLLEEN SEARCY

GETTING STARTED IN THE STORIES OF WOMEN

We have our best chance of understanding the stories of women if we overlay the Bible texts with important context. Below are context questions to address before you begin the study. For help answering these questions, you can watch my "Getting Started" video at colleensearcy.com/mmibteaching.

1. Why did God create women? (Gen. 1:26–31; 2:4–25)

2. What happened after God created the first woman? (Gen. 3)

3. In what style were these particular stories written and why does it matter? For help with these questions, see information about historical narratives in Tool 3 of the Tool Kit.[5]

4. Central themes to explore throughout this study:
    - What do we learn about God?
    - What do we learn about his view of women from the story of __________?
    - What do we learn about people?

1
SARAH AND HAGAR

Genesis 11:29–12:3; 16:1–16; 18:10–15; 21:1–21

SARAH AND HAGAR

Context for the Story of Sarah and Hagar

Where Are We in the Story of the Bible?

Turn to Tool 1 in the Tool Kit and place an *X* by the patriarchs. Pencil in the names of Sarah and Hagar there.

After the flood, Noah's sons spread out and established nations. Many years later, God called one man, Abraham, to begin a people for himself. Abraham was the first of the Hebrew patriarchs. The Hebrew people laid claim to the promised land based on the covenant God made with their first three patriarchs—Abraham, Isaac, and Jacob. Jacob's name was eventually changed to Israel, and his twelve sons gave rise to the twelve tribes of Israel.

Who Are Sarah and Hagar?

Genesis 16 and Genesis 21:1–21 are about Abraham's wife Sarah and her Egyptian servant Hagar. God had promised a son to Abraham and Sarah, but he was not in a hurry. In fact, God had promised Abraham so many descendants that they would be like the stars in the sky. Imagine how Abraham and Sarah felt, at eighty-six and seventy-six years old (16:16), and still childless. So Sarah made a plan, but the plan was hers, not God's. Read the passages to see their story unfold.

Helpful hint as you read Hagar's story: God's prophetic words about Ishmael becoming "a wild donkey of a man" in Genesis 16:12 sound like bad news rather than comforting news for Hagar. At this time in history, however, donkeys were considered noble, strong, and free (Job 39:4–8), creatures running wild and untamed in the wilderness. In other words, Ishmael would live as a free man, not as a slave like Hagar.

Genesis 11:29–12:3; 16:1–16; 18:10–15; 21:1–21

[11:29] And Abram and Nahor took wives. The name of Abram's wife was Sarai,
and the name of Nahor's wife, Milcah, the daughter of Haran the father of
Milcah and Iscah. [30] Now Sarai was barren; she had no child.

31 Terah took Abram his son and Lot the son of Haran, his grandson, and Sarai his daughter-in-law, his son Abram's wife, and they went forth together from Ur of the Chaldeans to go into the land of Canaan, but when they came to Haran, they settled there. 32 The days of Terah were 205 years, and Terah died in Haran.

12:1 Now the LORD said to Abram, "Go from your country and your kindred and your father's house to the land that I will show you. 2 And I will make of you a great nation, and I will bless you and make your name great, so that you will be a blessing. 3 I will bless those who bless you, and him who dishonors you I will curse, and in you all the families of the earth shall be blessed."

16:1 Now Sarai, Abram's wife, had borne him no children. She had a female Egyptian servant whose name was Hagar. 2 And Sarai said to Abram, "Behold now, the LORD has prevented me from bearing children. Go in to my servant; it may be that I shall obtain children by her." And Abram listened to the voice of Sarai. 3 So, after Abram had lived ten years in the land of Canaan, Sarai, Abram's wife, took Hagar the Egyptian, her servant, and gave her to Abram her husband as a wife. 4 And he went in to Hagar, and she conceived. And when she saw that she had conceived, she looked with contempt on her mistress. 5 And Sarai said to Abram, "May the wrong done to me be on you! I gave my servant to your embrace, and when she saw that she had conceived, she looked on me with contempt. May the LORD judge between you and me!" 6 But Abram said to Sarai, "Behold, your servant is in your power; do to her as you please." Then Sarai dealt harshly with her, and she fled from her.

7 The angel of the LORD found her by a spring of water in the wilderness, the spring on the way to Shur. 8 And he said, "Hagar, servant of Sarai, where have you come from and where are you going?" She said, "I am fleeing from my mistress Sarai." 9 The angel of the LORD said to her, "Return to your mistress and submit to her." 10 The angel of the LORD also said to her, "I will surely

multiply your offspring so that they cannot be numbered for multitude."
11 And the angel of the LORD said to her,

"Behold, you are pregnant
and shall bear a son.
You shall call his name Ishmael,
because the LORD has listened to your affliction.
12 He shall be a wild donkey of a man,
his hand against everyone
and everyone's hand against him,
and he shall dwell over against all his kinsmen."

13 So she called the name of the LORD who spoke to her, "You are a God of
seeing," for she said, "Truly here I have seen him who looks after me." 14 Therefore the well was called Beer-lahai-roi; it lies between Kadesh and Bered.
15 And Hagar bore Abram a son, and Abram called the name of his son,
whom Hagar bore, Ishmael. 16 Abram was eighty-six years old when Hagar
bore Ishmael to Abram.

18:10 The LORD said, "I will surely return to you about this time next year, and
Sarah your wife shall have a son." And Sarah was listening at the tent door
behind him. 11 Now Abraham and Sarah were old, advanced in years. The way
of women had ceased to be with Sarah. 12 So Sarah laughed to herself, saying,
"After I am worn out, and my lord is old, shall I have pleasure?" 13 The LORD
said to Abraham, "Why did Sarah laugh and say, 'Shall I indeed bear a child,
now that I am old?' 14 Is anything too hard for the LORD? At the appointed
time I will return to you, about this time next year, and Sarah shall have a
son." 15 But Sarah denied it, saying, "I did not laugh," for she was afraid. He
said, "No, but you did laugh."

[21:1] The LORD visited Sarah as he had said, and the LORD did to Sarah as he
had promised. [2] And Sarah conceived and bore Abraham a son in his old age
at the time of which God had spoken to him. [3] Abraham called the name of
his son who was born to him, whom Sarah bore him, Isaac. [4] And Abraham
circumcised his son Isaac when he was eight days old, as God had commanded him. [5] Abraham was a hundred years old when his son Isaac was
born to him. [6] And Sarah said, "God has made laughter for me; everyone who
hears will laugh over me." [7] And she said, "Who would have said to Abraham
that Sarah would nurse children? Yet I have borne him a son in his old age."

[8] And the child grew and was weaned. And Abraham made a great feast on
the day that Isaac was weaned. [9] But Sarah saw the son of Hagar the Egyptian,
whom she had borne to Abraham, laughing. [10] So she said to Abraham, "Cast
out this slave woman with her son, for the son of this slave woman shall not
be heir with my son Isaac." [11] And the thing was very displeasing to Abraham on account of his son. [12] But God said to Abraham, "Be not displeased
because of the boy and because of your slave woman. Whatever Sarah says
to you, do as she tells you, for through Isaac shall your offspring be named.
[13] And I will make a nation of the son of the slave woman also, because he
is your offspring." [14] So Abraham rose early in the morning and took bread
and a skin of water and gave it to Hagar, putting it on her shoulder, along
with the child, and sent her away. And she departed and wandered in the
wilderness of Beersheba.

[15] When the water in the skin was gone, she put the child under one of the
bushes. [16] Then she went and sat down opposite him a good way off, about
the distance of a bowshot, for she said, "Let me not look on the death of the
child." And as she sat opposite him, she lifted up her voice and wept. [17] And
God heard the voice of the boy, and the angel of God called to Hagar from
heaven and said to her, "What troubles you, Hagar? Fear not, for God has
heard the voice of the boy where he is. [18] Up! Lift up the boy, and hold him

fast with your hand, for I will make him into a great nation." [19] Then God
opened her eyes, and she saw a well of water. And she went and filled the
skin with water and gave the boy a drink. [20] And God was with the boy, and
he grew up. He lived in the wilderness and became an expert with the bow.
[21] He lived in the wilderness of Paran, and his mother took a wife for him
from the land of Egypt.

OBSERVE: WHAT DOES THE PASSAGE SAY?

Step 1: Setting and Summary

Key Characters and Locations

CHARACTERS:

- *Sarai*. Abram's wife, later named Sarah; she was barren.
- *Hagar*. Sarah's Egyptian servant.
- *Abram*. Sarai's husband, later named Abraham. He listened to Sarai's plan and slept with Hagar.
- *The angel of the Lord*. Found Hagar in the wilderness and spoke tenderly to her.

LOCATIONS:

Remember to reference the maps in Tool 2 of the Tool Kit.

- *Land of Canaan*. New dwelling place of Sarai and Abraham.
- *Beer-lahai-roi*. The spring of water in the wilderness where the Lord spoke to Hagar. This spring of water was on the way to Shur, which was between Canaan and Egypt.

Summary of the Passage

What Stood Out to You or Piqued Your Curiosity?

Step 2: Key Words and Phrases

Remember to look at the prompts on your Bible study bookmark as you observe the text.

- *"... had borne him no children." "... has prevented me from bearing children." "... that I shall obtain children."* (3 times)
- *Looked with contempt* (2 times). Dictionary definition of contempt: "the act of despising; lack of respect or reverence; disdain."[6]
- *"The angel of the Lord found her." "You are a God of seeing," "... him who looks after me."* NIV translation: "'You are the God who sees me,' for she said, 'I have now seen the One who sees me.'" (Gen. 16:13).

Remember to enjoy God and listen as you study. Move to a time of prayer after you observe, recording your prayer on the prayer pages in Tool 6.

NOTES

INTERPRET: WHAT DOES THE PASSAGE MEAN?

Step 3: What Was Hard to Understand?

Questions

- *Why was Sarai so angry when Hagar looked at her wrongly?*
- *Who was the angel of the Lord?*

Insights from Cross-References, Other Translations, and the Context

Remember that historical context is one of the greatest Bible study tools available. Keep asking the questions: Who wrote this? When did he write it? Where does this land in the whole story of the Bible? How would these words land on the ears of the original hearers?

- *Why was Sarai so angry when Hagar looked at her wrongly?* From cross-reference 1 Samuel 1:6: "And her rival used to provoke her grievously to irritate her, because the LORD had closed her womb." NIV translation of Genesis 16:4: "When she [Hagar] knew she was pregnant, she began to despise her mistress."
- *Who was the angel of the Lord?* Genesis 16:13: "She gave this name to the LORD who spoke to her: 'You are the God who sees me,' for she said, 'I have now seen the One who sees me.'" Hagar believed the Lord had spoken to her; a similar pattern is seen in cross-reference Genesis 22:11–17.

Remember to turn to the Questions for Further Thought and Discussion in Tool 7 for a deeper dive. Additional historical context is also given within the questions.

Step 4: What Did You Learn about God?

Refer to the attributes of God in Tool 4 if needed.

What did you learn about God's view of women?

Remember to enjoy God and listen as you study. Move to a time of prayer after you interpret, recording your prayer on the prayer pages in Tool 6.

NOTES

APPLY: HOW WILL YOU APPLY THE PASSAGE?

Step 5: What Did You Learn about People?

Others

Remember to look at the prompts on your Bible study bookmark as you apply the text.

Yourself

- *Is there a command to obey? An example to follow? A sin to confess? A warning to heed? An encouragement to receive?*
- *What action step will you take?*

Wrap Up: What Did You Discover in the Scriptures That Was Important to You?

Remember to enjoy God and listen as you study. Move to a time of prayer after you apply, recording your prayer on the prayer pages in Tool 6.

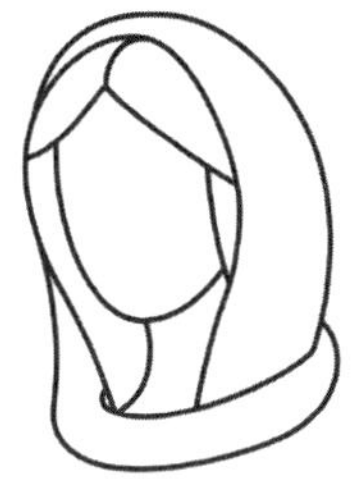

2
LEAH AND RACHEL

Genesis 29:1–35; 30:1–24; 49:28–33

LEAH AND RACHEL

Context for the Story of Leah and Rachel

Where Are We in the Story of the Bible?

Turn to Tool 1 in the Tool Kit and place an *X* by the Patriarchs, immediately to the right of the *X* for Sarah and Hagar. Pencil in the names of Leah and Rachel there.

God's promise to Abraham and Sarah came to pass, and Sarah had the unusual joy and challenge of having a baby as an elderly woman. The baby was named Isaac. Later, Isaac and his wife, Rebekah, also walked through the pain of infertility. Isaac prayed to the Lord for his wife, and Rebekah conceived famous twins, Jacob and Esau. The Scriptures tell us that these twin boys were already wrestling with one another in their mother's womb. Jacob was the younger twin, so by custom the birthright belonged to Esau. But God told Rebekah while she was pregnant that the older son would serve the younger. The Genesis account is clear that after Rebekah gave birth, she strongly favored Jacob, and Isaac favored Esau. Later, Rebekah devised a plan to ensure that her favorite would come out on top. Isaac had grown old and blind, so she dressed Jacob to smell and feel like his older brother, Esau. When it was time for Isaac to give the blessing to the firstborn, he was indeed tricked into giving the blessing to Jacob instead. Esau was so angry that he threatened to kill Jacob for this deception, and Rebekah made another plan to protect her favorite. Jacob was sent to her family's homeland, Haran, to find a wife (Gen. 27:41–45).

Helpful hint as you read their story: Mandrakes are a type of Mediterranean plant that were thought to have magical powers in the ancient East. Some thought that mandrakes increased fertility, while some thought the plant to be an aphrodisiac. Imagine the desperation of Leah and Rachel while you read Genesis 30:14–16.

Who Are Leah and Rachel?

Leah and Rachel were sisters, and they were Jacob's cousins. Both sisters became entangled in Jacob's complicated story. Read the passages to see their story unfold.

Genesis 29:1–35; 30:1–24; 49:28–33

29:1 Then Jacob went on his journey and came to the land of the people of the east. 2 As he looked, he saw a well in the field, and behold, three flocks of sheep lying beside it, for out of that well the flocks were watered. The stone on the well's mouth was large, 3 and when all the flocks were gathered there, the shepherds would roll the stone from the mouth of the well and water the sheep, and put the stone back in its place over the mouth of the well.

4 Jacob said to them, "My brothers, where do you come from?" They said, "We are from Haran." 5 He said to them, "Do you know Laban the son of Nahor?" They said, "We know him." 6 He said to them, "Is it well with him?" They said, "It is well; and see, Rachel his daughter is coming with the sheep!" 7 He said, "Behold, it is still high day; it is not time for the livestock to be gathered together. Water the sheep and go, pasture them." 8 But they said, "We cannot until all the flocks are gathered together and the stone is rolled from the mouth of the well; then we water the sheep."

9 While he was still speaking with them, Rachel came with her father's sheep, for she was a shepherdess. 10 Now as soon as Jacob saw Rachel the daughter of Laban his mother's brother, and the sheep of Laban his mother's brother, Jacob came near and rolled the stone from the well's mouth and watered the flock of Laban his mother's brother. 11 Then Jacob kissed Rachel and wept aloud. 12 And Jacob told Rachel that he was her father's kinsman, and that he was Rebekah's son, and she ran and told her father.

13 As soon as Laban heard the news about Jacob, his sister's son, he ran to meet him and embraced him and kissed him and brought him to his house. Jacob told Laban all these things, 14 and Laban said to him, "Surely you are my bone and my flesh!" And he stayed with him a month.

15 Then Laban said to Jacob, "Because you are my kinsman, should you therefore serve me for nothing? Tell me, what shall your wages be?" 16 Now

Laban had two daughters. The name of the older was Leah, and the name of the younger was Rachel. 17 Leah's eyes were weak, but Rachel was beautiful in form and appearance. 18 Jacob loved Rachel. And he said, "I will serve you seven years for your younger daughter Rachel." 19 Laban said, "It is better that I give her to you than that I should give her to any other man; stay with me." 20 So Jacob served seven years for Rachel, and they seemed to him but a few days because of the love he had for her.

21 Then Jacob said to Laban, "Give me my wife that I may go in to her, for my time is completed." 22 So Laban gathered together all the people of the place and made a feast. 23 But in the evening he took his daughter Leah and brought her to Jacob, and he went in to her. 24 (Laban gave his female servant Zilpah to his daughter Leah to be her servant.) 25 And in the morning, behold, it was Leah! And Jacob said to Laban, "What is this you have done to me? Did I not serve with you for Rachel? Why then have you deceived me?" 26 Laban said, "It is not so done in our country, to give the younger before the firstborn. 27 Complete the week of this one, and we will give you the other also in return for serving me another seven years." 28 Jacob did so, and completed her week. Then Laban gave him his daughter Rachel to be his wife. 29 (Laban gave his female servant Bilhah to his daughter Rachel to be her servant.) 30 So Jacob went in to Rachel also, and he loved Rachel more than Leah, and served Laban for another seven years.

31 When the LORD saw that Leah was hated, he opened her womb, but Rachel was barren. 32 And Leah conceived and bore a son, and she called his name Reuben, for she said, "Because the LORD has looked upon my affliction; for now my husband will love me." 33 She conceived again and bore a son, and said, "Because the LORD has heard that I am hated, he has given me this son also." And she called his name Simeon. 34 Again she conceived and bore a son, and said, "Now this time my husband will be attached to me, because I have borne him three sons." Therefore his name was called Levi. 35 And she

conceived again and bore a son, and said, "This time I will praise the LORD." Therefore she called his name Judah. Then she ceased bearing.

30:1 When Rachel saw that she bore Jacob no children, she envied her sister. She said to Jacob, "Give me children, or I shall die!" 2 Jacob's anger was kindled against Rachel, and he said, "Am I in the place of God, who has withheld from you the fruit of the womb?" 3 Then she said, "Here is my servant Bilhah; go in to her, so that she may give birth on my behalf, that even I may have children through her." 4 So she gave him her servant Bilhah as a wife, and Jacob went in to her. 5 And Bilhah conceived and bore Jacob a son. 6 Then Rachel said, "God has judged me, and has also heard my voice and given me a son." Therefore she called his name Dan. 7 Rachel's servant Bilhah conceived again and bore Jacob a second son. 8 Then Rachel said, "With mighty wrestlings I have wrestled with my sister and have prevailed." So she called his name Naphtali.

9 When Leah saw that she had ceased bearing children, she took her servant Zilpah and gave her to Jacob as a wife. 10 Then Leah's servant Zilpah bore Jacob a son. 11 And Leah said, "Good fortune has come!" so she called his name Gad. 12 Leah's servant Zilpah bore Jacob a second son. 13 And Leah said, "Happy am I! For women have called me happy." So she called his name Asher.

14 In the days of wheat harvest Reuben went and found mandrakes in the field and brought them to his mother Leah. Then Rachel said to Leah, "Please give me some of your son's mandrakes." 15 But she said to her, "Is it a small matter that you have taken away my husband? Would you take away my son's mandrakes also?" Rachel said, "Then he may lie with you tonight in exchange for your son's mandrakes." 16 When Jacob came from the field in the evening, Leah went out to meet him and said, "You must come in to me, for I have hired you with my son's mandrakes." So he lay with her that night. 17 And God listened to Leah, and she conceived and bore Jacob a fifth son.

18 Leah said, "God has given me my wages because I gave my servant to my
husband." So she called his name Issachar.
19 And Leah conceived again, and she bore Jacob a sixth son. 20 Then Leah
said, "God has endowed me with a good endowment; now my husband will
honor me, because I have borne him six sons." So she called his name Zebulun. 21 Afterward she bore a daughter and called her name Dinah.
22 Then God remembered Rachel, and God listened to her and opened her
womb. 23 She conceived and bore a son and said, "God has taken away my
reproach." 24 And she called his name Joseph, saying, "May the Lord add to
me another son!"

Much time passed. Genesis 49 is the recording of the end of Jacob's life.

49:28 All these are the twelve tribes of Israel. This is what their father said to
them as he blessed them, blessing each with the blessing suitable to him.
29 Then he commanded them and said to them, "I am to be gathered to my
people; bury me with my fathers in the cave that is in the field of Ephron the
Hittite, 30 in the cave that is in the field at Machpelah, to the east of Mamre, in
the land of Canaan, which Abraham bought with the field from Ephron the
Hittite to possess as a burying place. 31 There they buried Abraham and Sarah
his wife. There they buried Isaac and Rebekah his wife, and there I buried
Leah— 32 the field and the cave that is in it were bought from the Hittites."
33 When Jacob finished commanding his sons, he drew up his feet into the
bed and breathed his last and was gathered to his people.

OBSERVE: WHAT DOES THE PASSAGE SAY?

Step 1: Setting and Summary

Key Characters and Locations

CHARACTERS:

LOCATIONS:

Summary of the Passage

What Stood Out to You or Piqued Your Curiosity?

Step 2: Key Words and Phrases

NOTES

INTERPRET: WHAT DOES THE PASSAGE MEAN?

Step 3: What Was Hard to Understand?

Questions

Insights from Cross-References, Other Translations, and the Context

Step 4: What Did You Learn about God?

Refer to the attributes of God in Tool 4 if needed.

What did you learn about God's view of women?

NOTES

APPLY: HOW WILL YOU APPLY THE PASSAGE?

Step 5: What Did You Learn about People?

Others

Yourself

Wrap Up: What Did You Discover in the Scriptures That Was Important to You?

3
WOMEN IN EXODUS

Exodus 1:1–22; 2:1–10

WOMEN IN EXODUS

Context for the Stories of Women in Exodus

Where Are We in the Story of the Bible?

Turn to Tool 1 in the Tool Kit and place an *X* by Egypt. Pencil in the names of the midwives Shiphrah and Puah and Moses's mother and sister, Jochebed and Miriam. Also add Pharaoh's daughter. It's a good thing there is a lot of space!

The covenant promises of God continued through the generations of the patriarchs, from Abraham to Isaac, to Jacob (whose name was changed to Israel), and then to Judah. Jacob's twelve sons gave rise to the twelve tribes of Israel. Joseph was Jacob's favorite son, which incited jealousy and hatred in the other sons. The brothers of Joseph sold him to an Ishmaelite caravan on their way to Egypt. But what the brothers had meant for his harm, God meant for good (Gen. 50:20). Joseph was eventually placed over all of Egypt, second only to Pharaoh. When famine swept the land of Canaan, the nation of Israel (Jacob's family, seventy in number) moved to Egypt and reunited with Joseph. Because of Joseph's favor with Pharaoh, Pharaoh gave Israel the land of Goshen in Egypt. The Israelites stayed in Egypt for 430 years, growing in number and strength.

Who Are These Five Women in the Book of Exodus?

Jochebed was Moses's mother (Num. 26:59), and Miriam was his sister. Two Hebrew midwives, Shiphrah and Puah, are also introduced, and Pharaoh's daughter. All acted courageously to preserve life. Later in Exodus (15:20), we see Miriam the prophetess leading women in worship after the Israelites were saved from the hand of the Egyptians. Read the passages to see their stories unfold.

Exodus 1:1–22; 2:1–10

[1:1] These are the names of the sons of Israel who came to Egypt with Jacob, each
with his household: [2] Reuben, Simeon, Levi, and Judah, [3] Issachar, Zebulun,
and Benjamin, [4] Dan and Naphtali, Gad and Asher. [5] All the descendants of

Jacob were seventy persons; Joseph was already in Egypt. 6 Then Joseph died, and all his brothers and all that generation. 7 But the people of Israel were fruitful and increased greatly; they multiplied and grew exceedingly strong, so that the land was filled with them.

8 Now there arose a new king over Egypt, who did not know Joseph. 9 And he said to his people, "Behold, the people of Israel are too many and too mighty for us. 10 Come, let us deal shrewdly with them, lest they multiply, and, if war breaks out, they join our enemies and fight against us and escape from the land." 11 Therefore they set taskmasters over them to afflict them with heavy burdens. They built for Pharaoh store cities, Pithom and Raamses. 12 But the more they were oppressed, the more they multiplied and the more they spread abroad. And the Egyptians were in dread of the people of Israel. 13 So they ruthlessly made the people of Israel work as slaves 14 and made their lives bitter with hard service, in mortar and brick, and in all kinds of work in the field. In all their work they ruthlessly made them work as slaves.

15 Then the king of Egypt said to the Hebrew midwives, one of whom was named Shiphrah and the other Puah, 16 "When you serve as midwife to the Hebrew women and see them on the birthstool, if it is a son, you shall kill him, but if it is a daughter, she shall live." 17 But the midwives feared God and did not do as the king of Egypt commanded them, but let the male children live. 18 So the king of Egypt called the midwives and said to them, "Why have you done this, and let the male children live?" 19 The midwives said to Pharaoh, "Because the Hebrew women are not like the Egyptian women, for they are vigorous and give birth before the midwife comes to them." 20 So God dealt well with the midwives. And the people multiplied and grew very strong. 21 And because the midwives feared God, he gave them families. 22 Then Pharaoh commanded all his people, "Every son that is born to the Hebrews you shall cast into the Nile, but you shall let every daughter live."

2:1 Now a man from the house of Levi went and took as his wife a Levite woman. 2 The woman conceived and bore a son, and when she saw that he was a fine child, she hid him three months. 3 When she could hide him no longer, she took for him a basket made of bulrushes and daubed it with bitumen and pitch. She put the child in it and placed it among the reeds by the river bank. 4 And his sister stood at a distance to know what would be done to him. 5 Now the daughter of Pharaoh came down to bathe at the river, while her young women walked beside the river. She saw the basket among the reeds and sent her servant woman, and she took it. 6 When she opened it, she saw the child, and behold, the baby was crying. She took pity on him and said, “This is one of the Hebrews’ children.” 7 Then his sister said to Pharaoh’s daughter, “Shall I go and call you a nurse from the Hebrew women to nurse the child for you?” 8 And Pharaoh’s daughter said to her, “Go.” So the girl went and called the child’s mother. 9 And Pharaoh’s daughter said to her, “Take this child away and nurse him for me, and I will give you your wages.” So the woman took the child and nursed him. 10 When the child grew older, she brought him to Pharaoh’s daughter, and he became her son. She named him Moses, “Because,” she said, “I drew him out of the water.”

OBSERVE: WHAT DOES THE PASSAGE SAY?

Step 1: Setting and Summary

Key Characters and Locations

CHARACTERS:

LOCATIONS:

Summary of the Passage

What Stood Out to You or Piqued Your Curiosity?

Step 2: Key Words and Phrases

NOTES

INTERPRET: WHAT DOES THE PASSAGE MEAN?

Step 3: What Was Hard to Understand?

Questions

Insights from Cross-References, Other Translations, and the Context

Step 4: What Did You Learn about God?

Refer to the attributes of God in Tool 4 if needed.

What did you learn about God's view of women?

NOTES

APPLY: HOW WILL YOU APPLY THE PASSAGE?

Step 5: What Did You Learn about People?

Others

Yourself

Wrap Up: What Did You Discover in the Scriptures That Was Important to You?

4
DEBORAH AND JAEL

Judges 2:11–23; 4:1–24; 5:1–9, 19–31

DEBORAH AND JAEL

Context for the Story of Deborah and Jael

Where Are We in the Story of the Bible?

Turn to Tool 1 in the Tool Kit and place an *X* after "Promised Land Entered." Pencil in the names of Deborah and Jael there.

After the Israelites had lived in Egypt 430 years, God raised up a deliverer, Moses. Moses led them out of Egypt and out of slavery (the exodus). His successor, Joshua, led the Israelites into the promised land. Sadly, the Israelites only partially conquered the Canaanites in the promised land despite the fact that the Lord had given their enemies into their hands. This brings us to the book of Judges.

There is a recurring pattern in the book of Judges:

- The Israelites abandoned the God of their fathers and served false gods.
- God gave them over to their enemies.
- The Israelites were oppressed and called out to God for help.
- The Lord raised up a judge to rescue them.
- They became complacent, worshiping other gods again.

And the pattern repeated, again and again.

Who Are Deborah and Jael?

Deborah was a prophetess and one of the judges that God raised up to deliver Israel from oppression. Deborah, Barak, and Jael led the charge against the evil King Jabin of Canaan and his wicked general, Sisera.

Helpful hints as you read their stories: Pay special attention to Judges 5:4 and 5:21 for hints of how the Canaanite troops were defeated. Kishon is the river where Sisera's troops and Barak's troops battled in the northern part of Israel. You can find it on the map titled "The Tribal Allotments of Israel" in Tool 2 of the Tool Kit.

The story of Jael is jarring. The historical context is important in understanding why her role was honorable and pleasing to the Lord. Pay special attention to verses 6–9 in chapter 5 and verses 28–30 for insight into what life was like for the Israelites under the oppression of King Jabin and his general, Sisera.

Judges 2:11–23; 4:1–24; 5:1–9, 19–31

2:11 And the people of Israel did what was evil in the sight of the LORD and served the Baals. 12 And they abandoned the LORD, the God of their fathers, who had brought them out of the land of Egypt. They went after other gods, from among the gods of the peoples who were around them, and bowed down to them. And they provoked the LORD to anger. 13 They abandoned the LORD and served the Baals and the Ashtaroth. 14 So the anger of the LORD was kindled against Israel, and he gave them over to plunderers, who plundered them. And he sold them into the hand of their surrounding enemies, so that they could no longer withstand their enemies. 15 Whenever they marched out, the hand of the LORD was against them for harm, as the LORD had warned, and as the LORD had sworn to them. And they were in terrible distress.

16 Then the LORD raised up judges, who saved them out of the hand of those who plundered them. 17 Yet they did not listen to their judges, for they whored after other gods and bowed down to them. They soon turned aside from the way in which their fathers had walked, who had obeyed the commandments of the LORD, and they did not do so. 18 Whenever the LORD raised up judges for them, the LORD was with the judge, and he saved them from the hand of their enemies all the days of the judge. For the LORD was moved to pity by their groaning because of those who afflicted and oppressed them. 19 But whenever the judge died, they turned back and were more corrupt than their fathers, going after other gods, serving them and bowing down to them. They did not drop any of their practices or their stubborn ways. 20 So the anger of the LORD was kindled against

Israel, and he said, "Because this people have transgressed my covenant that I commanded their fathers and have not obeyed my voice, [21] I will no longer drive out before them any of the nations that Joshua left when he died, [22] in order to test Israel by them, whether they will take care to walk in the way of the LORD as their fathers did, or not." [23] So the LORD left those nations, not driving them out quickly, and he did not give them into the hand of Joshua.

[4:1] And the people of Israel again did what was evil in the sight of the LORD after Ehud died. [2] And the LORD sold them into the hand of Jabin king of Canaan, who reigned in Hazor. The commander of his army was Sisera, who lived in Harosheth-hagoyim. [3] Then the people of Israel cried out to the LORD for help, for he had 900 chariots of iron and he oppressed the people of Israel cruelly for twenty years.

[4] Now Deborah, a prophetess, the wife of Lappidoth, was judging Israel at that time. [5] She used to sit under the palm of Deborah between Ramah and Bethel in the hill country of Ephraim, and the people of Israel came up to her for judgment. [6] She sent and summoned Barak the son of Abinoam from Kedesh-naphtali and said to him, "Has not the LORD, the God of Israel, commanded you, 'Go, gather your men at Mount Tabor, taking 10,000 from the people of Naphtali and the people of Zebulun. [7] And I will draw out Sisera, the general of Jabin's army, to meet you by the river Kishon with his chariots and his troops, and I will give him into your hand'?" [8] Barak said to her, "If you will go with me, I will go, but if you will not go with me, I will not go." [9] And she said, "I will surely go with you. Nevertheless, the road on which you are going will not lead to your glory, for the LORD will sell Sisera into the hand of a woman." Then Deborah arose and went with Barak to Kedesh. [10] And Barak called out Zebulun and Naphtali to Kedesh. And 10,000 men went up at his heels, and Deborah went up with him.

11 Now Heber the Kenite had separated from the Kenites, the descendants
of Hobab the father-in-law of Moses, and had pitched his tent as far away as
the oak in Zaanannim, which is near Kedesh.

12 When Sisera was told that Barak the son of Abinoam had gone up to
Mount Tabor, 13 Sisera called out all his chariots, 900 chariots of iron, and all
the men who were with him, from Harosheth-hagoyim to the river Kishon.
14 And Deborah said to Barak, "Up! For this is the day in which the LORD
has given Sisera into your hand. Does not the LORD go out before you?"
So Barak went down from Mount Tabor with 10,000 men following him.
15 And the LORD routed Sisera and all his chariots and all his army before
Barak by the edge of the sword. And Sisera got down from his chariot and
fled away on foot. 16 And Barak pursued the chariots and the army to Harosheth-hagoyim, and all the army of Sisera fell by the edge of the sword;
not a man was left.

17 But Sisera fled away on foot to the tent of Jael, the wife of Heber the
Kenite, for there was peace between Jabin the king of Hazor and the house of
Heber the Kenite. 18 And Jael came out to meet Sisera and said to him, "Turn
aside, my lord; turn aside to me; do not be afraid." So he turned aside to her
into the tent, and she covered him with a rug. 19 And he said to her, "Please
give me a little water to drink, for I am thirsty." So she opened a skin of milk
and gave him a drink and covered him. 20 And he said to her, "Stand at the
opening of the tent, and if any man comes and asks you, 'Is anyone here?'
say, 'No.'" 21 But Jael the wife of Heber took a tent peg, and took a hammer
in her hand. Then she went softly to him and drove the peg into his temple
until it went down into the ground while he was lying fast asleep from wea-
riness. So he died. 22 And behold, as Barak was pursuing Sisera, Jael went
out to meet him and said to him, "Come, and I will show you the man whom
you are seeking." So he went in to her tent, and there lay Sisera dead, with
the tent peg in his temple.

[23] So on that day God subdued Jabin the king of Canaan before the people
of Israel. [24] And the hand of the people of Israel pressed harder and harder
against Jabin the king of Canaan, until they destroyed Jabin king of Canaan.
[5:1] Then sang Deborah and Barak the son of Abinoam on that day:

2 "That the leaders took the lead in Israel,
that the people offered themselves willingly,
bless the LORD!

3 "Hear, O kings; give ear, O princes;
to the LORD I will sing;
I will make melody to the LORD, the God of Israel.

4 "LORD, when you went out from Seir,
when you marched from the region of Edom,
the earth trembled
and the heavens dropped,
yes, the clouds dropped water.
5 The mountains quaked before the LORD,
even Sinai before the LORD, the God of Israel.

6 "In the days of Shamgar, son of Anath,
in the days of Jael, the highways were abandoned,
and travelers kept to the byways.
7 The villagers ceased in Israel;
they ceased to be until I arose;
I, Deborah, arose as a mother in Israel.
8 When new gods were chosen,
then war was in the gates.

Was shield or spear to be seen
    among forty thousand in Israel?
9 My heart goes out to the commanders of Israel
    who offered themselves willingly among the people.
    Bless the LORD. . . .

19 "The kings came, they fought;
    then fought the kings of Canaan,
at Taanach, by the waters of Megiddo;
    they got no spoils of silver.
20 From heaven the stars fought,
    from their courses they fought against Sisera.
21 The torrent Kishon swept them away,
    the ancient torrent, the torrent Kishon.
    March on, my soul, with might!

22 "Then loud beat the horses' hoofs
    with the galloping, galloping of his steeds.

23 "Curse Meroz, says the angel of the LORD,
    curse its inhabitants thoroughly,
because they did not come to the help of the LORD,
    to the help of the LORD against the mighty.

24 "Most blessed of women be Jael,
    the wife of Heber the Kenite,
    of tent-dwelling women most blessed.
25 He asked for water and she gave him milk;
    she brought him curds in a noble's bowl.

26 She sent her hand to the tent peg
    and her right hand to the workmen's mallet;
she struck Sisera;
    she crushed his head;
    she shattered and pierced his temple.
27 Between her feet
    he sank, he fell, he lay still;
between her feet
    he sank, he fell;
where he sank,
    there he fell—dead.

28 "Out of the window she peered,
    the mother of Sisera wailed through the lattice:
'Why is his chariot so long in coming?
    Why tarry the hoofbeats of his chariots?'
29 Her wisest princesses answer,
    indeed, she answers herself,
30 'Have they not found and divided the spoil?—
    A womb or two for every man;
spoil of dyed materials for Sisera,
    spoil of dyed materials embroidered,
    two pieces of dyed work embroidered for the neck as spoil?'

31 "So may all your enemies perish, O Lord!
    But your friends be like the sun as he rises in his might."

And the land had rest for forty years.

OBSERVE: WHAT DOES THE PASSAGE SAY?

Step 1: Setting and Summary

Key Characters and Locations

CHARACTERS:

LOCATIONS:

Summary of the Passage

What Stood Out to You or Piqued Your Curiosity?

Step 2: Key Words and Phrases

NOTES

INTERPRET: WHAT DOES THE PASSAGE MEAN?

Step 3: What Was Hard to Understand?

Questions

Insights from Cross-References, Other Translations, and the Context

Step 4: What Did You Learn about God?

Refer to the attributes of God in Tool 4 if needed.

What did you learn about God's view of women?

NOTES

APPLY: HOW WILL YOU APPLY THE PASSAGE?

Step 5: What Did You Learn about People?

Others

Yourself

Wrap Up: What Did You Discover in the Scriptures That Was Important to You?

5
ELIZABETH AND MARY

Luke 1:1–66

ELIZABETH AND MARY

Context for the Story of Elizabeth and Mary

Where Are We in the Story of the Bible?

Turn to Tool 1 in the Tool Kit and place an *X* right before the incarnation. Pencil in the names of Elizabeth and Mary there.

At the end of the period of the kings and afterward, the Jews were conquered and oppressed by the Assyrians, the Babylonians, the Medes and Persians, the Greeks, and then the Romans. God did not speak through prophets for four hundred years. Poverty and injustice were common under Roman occupation and rule. The afflicted, yet chosen, people of God awaited their leader who had been promised centuries before by the prophets of the Old Testament. This promised leader, the Messiah, was to rescue them and establish a new kingdom. As their king, he would establish peace and enact justice. The Jews expected immediate relief upon the Messiah's arrival, and they anticipated immediate overthrow. Yet they overlooked the prophecies that also spoke of this king as a suffering servant who would be rejected by men. The Messiah did come, just not in the way the Jews expected. But he was exactly who they needed. He came to oppressed, poverty-stricken people as a poor and lowly baby.

Who Are Elizabeth and Mary?

Elizabeth was an elderly woman who had not been able to have children. She was married to Zechariah, one of many Jewish priests. Priests were divided into twenty-four divisions, and Zechariah was chosen by lot among his division (the division of Abijah) to serve in the temple sanctuary and burn incense on behalf of the Jewish people. While serving in the temple, he was visited by the angel Gabriel, who announced that Elizabeth would become the mother of John the Baptist, who would be the herald of the long-awaited Messiah. Elizabeth was Mary's much-older cousin. Mary was a virgin and young teenager who also received a visit and an announcement from Gabriel: she would become the mother of the Messiah, Jesus Christ. Read the passage to see their story unfold.

Luke 1:1–66

1 Inasmuch as many have undertaken to compile a narrative of the things that
have been accomplished among us, 2 just as those who from the beginning
were eyewitnesses and ministers of the word have delivered them to us, 3 it
seemed good to me also, having followed all things closely for some time
past, to write an orderly account for you, most excellent Theophilus, 4 that
you may have certainty concerning the things you have been taught.

5 In the days of Herod, king of Judea, there was a priest named Zechariah,
of the division of Abijah. And he had a wife from the daughters of Aaron,
and her name was Elizabeth. 6 And they were both righteous before God,
walking blamelessly in all the commandments and statutes of the Lord. 7 But
they had no child, because Elizabeth was barren, and both were advanced
in years.

8 Now while he was serving as priest before God when his division was
on duty, 9 according to the custom of the priesthood, he was chosen by lot to
enter the temple of the Lord and burn incense. 10 And the whole multitude of
the people were praying outside at the hour of incense. 11 And there appeared
to him an angel of the Lord standing on the right side of the altar of incense.
12 And Zechariah was troubled when he saw him, and fear fell upon him. 13 But
the angel said to him, "Do not be afraid, Zechariah, for your prayer has been
heard, and your wife Elizabeth will bear you a son, and you shall call his name
John. 14 And you will have joy and gladness, and many will rejoice at his birth,
15 for he will be great before the Lord. And he must not drink wine or strong
drink, and he will be filled with the Holy Spirit, even from his mother's womb.
16 And he will turn many of the children of Israel to the Lord their God, 17 and
he will go before him in the spirit and power of Elijah, to turn the hearts of
the fathers to the children, and the disobedient to the wisdom of the just, to
make ready for the Lord a people prepared."

18 And Zechariah said to the angel, "How shall I know this? For I am an old
man, and my wife is advanced in years." 19 And the angel answered him, "I am
Gabriel. I stand in the presence of God, and I was sent to speak to you and
to bring you this good news. 20 And behold, you will be silent and unable to
speak until the day that these things take place, because you did not believe
my words, which will be fulfilled in their time." 21 And the people were waiting
for Zechariah, and they were wondering at his delay in the temple. 22 And when
he came out, he was unable to speak to them, and they realized that he had
seen a vision in the temple. And he kept making signs to them and remained
mute. 23 And when his time of service was ended, he went to his home.

24 After these days his wife Elizabeth conceived, and for five months she
kept herself hidden, saying, 25 "Thus the Lord has done for me in the days
when he looked on me, to take away my reproach among people."

26 In the sixth month the angel Gabriel was sent from God to a city of
Galilee named Nazareth, 27 to a virgin betrothed to a man whose name was
Joseph, of the house of David. And the virgin's name was Mary. 28 And he
came to her and said, "Greetings, O favored one, the Lord is with you!" 29 But
she was greatly troubled at the saying, and tried to discern what sort of
greeting this might be. 30 And the angel said to her, "Do not be afraid, Mary,
for you have found favor with God. 31 And behold, you will conceive in your
womb and bear a son, and you shall call his name Jesus. 32 He will be great
and will be called the Son of the Most High. And the Lord God will give
to him the throne of his father David, 33 and he will reign over the house of
Jacob forever, and of his kingdom there will be no end."

34 And Mary said to the angel, "How will this be, since I am a virgin?"

35 And the angel answered her, "The Holy Spirit will come upon you, and
the power of the Most High will overshadow you; therefore the child to be
born will be called holy—the Son of God. 36 And behold, your relative Elizabeth
in her old age has also conceived a son, and this is the sixth month with her

who was called barren. 37 For nothing will be impossible with God." 38 And
Mary said, "Behold, I am the servant of the Lord; let it be to me according to
your word." And the angel departed from her.

39 In those days Mary arose and went with haste into the hill country, to
a town in Judah, 40 and she entered the house of Zechariah and greeted
Elizabeth. 41 And when Elizabeth heard the greeting of Mary, the baby
leaped in her womb. And Elizabeth was filled with the Holy Spirit, 42 and she
exclaimed with a loud cry, "Blessed are you among women, and blessed is
the fruit of your womb! 43 And why is this granted to me that the mother of
my Lord should come to me? 44 For behold, when the sound of your greeting came to my ears, the baby in my womb leaped for joy. 45 And blessed
is she who believed that there would be a fulfillment of what was spoken
to her from the Lord."

46 And Mary said,

"My soul magnifies the Lord,
47 and my spirit rejoices in God my Savior,
48 for he has looked on the humble estate of his servant.
For behold, from now on all generations will call me blessed;
49 for he who is mighty has done great things for me,
and holy is his name.
50 And his mercy is for those who fear him
from generation to generation.
51 He has shown strength with his arm;
he has scattered the proud in the thoughts of their hearts;
52 he has brought down the mighty from their thrones
and exalted those of humble estate;
53 he has filled the hungry with good things,
and the rich he has sent away empty.

54 He has helped his servant Israel,
in remembrance of his mercy,
55 as he spoke to our fathers,
to Abraham and to his offspring forever."

56 And Mary remained with her about three months and returned to her home.
57 Now the time came for Elizabeth to give birth, and she bore a son. 58 And
her neighbors and relatives heard that the Lord had shown great mercy to her,
and they rejoiced with her. 59 And on the eighth day they came to circumcise
the child. And they would have called him Zechariah after his father, 60 but
his mother answered, "No; he shall be called John." 61 And they said to her,
"None of your relatives is called by this name." 62 And they made signs to
his father, inquiring what he wanted him to be called. 63 And he asked for a
writing tablet and wrote, "His name is John." And they all wondered. 64 And
immediately his mouth was opened and his tongue loosed, and he spoke,
blessing God. 65 And fear came on all their neighbors. And all these things
were talked about through all the hill country of Judea, 66 and all who heard
them laid them up in their hearts, saying, "What then will this child be?" For
the hand of the Lord was with him.

OBSERVE: WHAT DOES THE PASSAGE SAY?

Step 1: Setting and Summary

Key Characters and Locations

CHARACTERS:

LOCATIONS:

Summary of the Passage

What Stood Out to You or Piqued Your Curiosity?

Step 2: Key Words and Phrases

NOTES

INTERPRET: WHAT DOES THE PASSAGE MEAN?

Step 3: What Was Hard to Understand?

Questions

Insights from Cross-References, Other Translations, and the Context

Step 4: What Did You Learn about God?

Refer to the attributes of God in Tool 4 if needed.

What did you learn about God's view of women?

NOTES

APPLY: HOW WILL YOU APPLY THE PASSAGE?

Step 5: What Did You Learn about People?

Others

Yourself

Wrap Up: What Did You Discover in the Scriptures That Was Important to You?

6

ANNA AND TABITHA

Luke 2:22–38; Acts 9:36–43

ANNA AND TABITHA

Context for the Stories of Anna and Tabitha

Where Are We in the Story of the Bible?

Turn to Tool 1 in the Tool Kit and place an *X* right after the incarnation. Pencil in Anna's name there. Then place another *X* by the church. Pencil in Tabitha's name there.

Context for Anna's Story

In the second chapter of the Gospel of Luke, we read that the long-awaited Messiah had come to earth at last! When baby Jesus was eight days old, his devout Jewish parents took him to the temple in Jerusalem to be presented to the Lord, according to the law of Moses (Ex. 13:1–2, 11–16; Lev. 12:1–8). God ordained that a faithful elderly man, Simeon, and a faithful elderly woman, Anna, would see the Christ child at the temple and testify to the fact that the Messiah had come.

Context for Tabitha's Story

At the beginning of the book of Acts, we read that the resurrected Son of God ascended from earth into heaven, and the Spirit of God descended to earth at Pentecost. The church was established, and the number of disciples of Jesus Christ increased greatly. Tabitha was one of Christ's disciples in Joppa. You can find Joppa on the map titled "Palestine under Roman Rule" in Tool 2 of the Tool Kit. Peter was building the church throughout Judea, Galilee, and Samaria. Paul's ministry was primarily to the Gentiles, expanding the church from Antioch to Rome.

Who Are Anna and Tabitha?

Anna was a prophetess who lived most of her life as a widow. She was fruitful through her ministry at the temple, praying and fasting daily. Tabitha was fruitful through her good works, particularly her ministry to widows. Throughout the Scriptures, God instructed his people again and again to care for widows. Tabitha entered into God's special attention to widows not only by meeting their needs but also by making them new clothes. Read the passages to see their stories unfold.

Luke 2:22–38; Acts 9:36–43

2:22 And when the time came for their purification according to the Law of
Moses, they brought him up to Jerusalem to present him to the Lord 23 (as
it is written in the Law of the Lord, "Every male who first opens the womb
shall be called holy to the Lord") 24 and to offer a sacrifice according to what
is said in the Law of the Lord, "a pair of turtledoves, or two young pigeons."
25 Now there was a man in Jerusalem, whose name was Simeon, and this man
was righteous and devout, waiting for the consolation of Israel, and the Holy
Spirit was upon him. 26 And it had been revealed to him by the Holy Spirit
that he would not see death before he had seen the Lord's Christ. 27 And he
came in the Spirit into the temple, and when the parents brought in the child
Jesus, to do for him according to the custom of the Law, 28 he took him up in
his arms and blessed God and said,

29 "Lord, now you are letting your servant depart in peace,
according to your word;
30 for my eyes have seen your salvation
31 that you have prepared in the presence of all peoples,
32 a light for revelation to the Gentiles,
and for glory to your people Israel."

33 And his father and his mother marveled at what was said about him.
34 And Simeon blessed them and said to Mary his mother, "Behold, this child
is appointed for the fall and rising of many in Israel, and for a sign that is
opposed 35 (and a sword will pierce through your own soul also), so that
thoughts from many hearts may be revealed."

36 And there was a prophetess, Anna, the daughter of Phanuel, of the tribe of
Asher. She was advanced in years, having lived with her husband seven years
from when she was a virgin, 37 and then as a widow until she was eighty-four.
She did not depart from the temple, worshiping with fasting and prayer night
and day. 38 And coming up at that very hour she began to give thanks to God
and to speak of him to all who were waiting for the redemption of Jerusalem.

9:36 Now there was in Joppa a disciple named Tabitha, which, translated, means
Dorcas. She was full of good works and acts of charity. 37 In those days she
became ill and died, and when they had washed her, they laid her in an upper
room. 38 Since Lydda was near Joppa, the disciples, hearing that Peter was
there, sent two men to him, urging him, "Please come to us without delay."
39 So Peter rose and went with them. And when he arrived, they took him to the
upper room. All the widows stood beside him weeping and showing tunics
and other garments that Dorcas made while she was with them. 40 But Peter
put them all outside, and knelt down and prayed; and turning to the body he
said, "Tabitha, arise." And she opened her eyes, and when she saw Peter she
sat up. 41 And he gave her his hand and raised her up. Then, calling the saints
and widows, he presented her alive. 42 And it became known throughout all
Joppa, and many believed in the Lord. 43 And he stayed in Joppa for many
days with one Simon, a tanner.

OBSERVE: WHAT DOES THE PASSAGE SAY?

Step 1: Setting and Summary

Key Characters and Locations

CHARACTERS:

LOCATIONS:

Summary of the Passage

What Stood Out to You or Piqued Your Curiosity?

Step 2: Key Words and Phrases

NOTES

INTERPRET: WHAT DOES THE PASSAGE MEAN?

Step 3: What Was Hard to Understand?

Questions

Insights from Cross-References, Other Translations, and the Context

Step 4: What Did You Learn about God?

Refer to the attributes of God in Tool 4 if needed.

What did you learn about God's view of women?

NOTES

APPLY: HOW WILL YOU APPLY THE PASSAGE?

Step 5: What Did You Learn about People?

Others

Yourself

Wrap Up: What Did You Discover in the Scriptures That Was Important to You?

7
MARTHA AND MARY

Luke 10:38–42; John 11:1–46; 12:1–8

MARTHA AND MARY

Context for the Stories of Martha and Mary

Where Are We in the Story of the Bible?

Turn to Tool 1 in the Tool Kit and place an *X* before the crucifixion, resurrection, and ascension. Pencil in the names of Martha and Mary there. Be sure to leave a little room for other names in the study.

During his later ministry, there was rising opposition toward Jesus among the Jewish religious leaders. Jesus knew his time was coming to be arrested and crucified, and he set his face toward Jerusalem (Luke 9:51). Martha and Mary welcomed Jesus as a guest in their home.

Who are Martha and Mary?

Martha and Mary were sisters. They lived in the village of Bethany, outside of Jerusalem. They had a brother named Lazarus. All three siblings were friends of Jesus.

- Helpful hint as you read their story in Luke 10: Jewish custom highly regarded hospitality, and hosting was a cultural expectation. The word *distracted* in the original language means to be cumbered, burdened, or dragged away.

- Helpful hint as you read their story in John 11: It was significant that Lazarus had been dead for four days. Jewish mysticism taught that a deceased person's spirit remained around the body for up to three days before departing. According to these ancient beliefs, the spirit left the body completely and went to Sheol or Hades on the fourth day. Also, by the fourth day in Israel's climate, advanced decay would have set in, destroying the body, and the stench would have been overwhelming. When Jesus called Lazarus to life from the dead, the timing discounted the superstitious beliefs that Lazarus had not been fully dead.

Read the passages to see their story unfold.

Luke 10:38–42; John 11:1–46; 12:1–8

10:38 Now as they went on their way, Jesus entered a village. And a woman named Martha welcomed him into her house. 39 And she had a sister called Mary, who sat at the Lord's feet and listened to his teaching. 40 But Martha was distracted with much serving. And she went up to him and said, "Lord, do you not care that my sister has left me to serve alone? Tell her then to help me." 41 But the Lord answered her, "Martha, Martha, you are anxious and troubled about many things, 42 but one thing is necessary. Mary has chosen the good portion, which will not be taken away from her."

11:1 Now a certain man was ill, Lazarus of Bethany, the village of Mary and her sister Martha. 2 It was Mary who anointed the Lord with ointment and wiped his feet with her hair, whose brother Lazarus was ill. 3 So the sisters sent to him, saying, "Lord, he whom you love is ill." 4 But when Jesus heard it he said, "This illness does not lead to death. It is for the glory of God, so that the Son of God may be glorified through it."

5 Now Jesus loved Martha and her sister and Lazarus. 6 So, when he heard that Lazarus was ill, he stayed two days longer in the place where he was. 7 Then after this he said to the disciples, "Let us go to Judea again." 8 The disciples said to him, "Rabbi, the Jews were just now seeking to stone you, and are you going there again?" 9 Jesus answered, "Are there not twelve hours in the day? If anyone walks in the day, he does not stumble, because he sees the light of this world. 10 But if anyone walks in the night, he stumbles, because the light is not in him." 11 After saying these things, he said to them, "Our friend Lazarus has fallen asleep, but I go to awaken him." 12 The disciples said to him, "Lord, if he has fallen asleep, he will recover." 13 Now Jesus had spoken of his death, but they thought that he meant taking rest in sleep. 14 Then Jesus told them plainly, "Lazarus has died, 15 and for your sake I am glad that I was not

there, so that you may believe. But let us go to him." 16 So Thomas, called the Twin, said to his fellow disciples, "Let us also go, that we may die with him."

17 Now when Jesus came, he found that Lazarus had already been in the tomb four days. 18 Bethany was near Jerusalem, about two miles off, 19 and many of the Jews had come to Martha and Mary to console them concerning their brother. 20 So when Martha heard that Jesus was coming, she went and met him, but Mary remained seated in the house. 21 Martha said to Jesus, "Lord, if you had been here, my brother would not have died. 22 But even now I know that whatever you ask from God, God will give you." 23 Jesus said to her, "Your brother will rise again." 24 Martha said to him, "I know that he will rise again in the resurrection on the last day." 25 Jesus said to her, "I am the resurrection and the life. Whoever believes in me, though he die, yet shall he live, 26 and everyone who lives and believes in me shall never die. Do you believe this?" 27 She said to him, "Yes, Lord; I believe that you are the Christ, the Son of God, who is coming into the world."

28 When she had said this, she went and called her sister Mary, saying in private, "The Teacher is here and is calling for you." 29 And when she heard it, she rose quickly and went to him. 30 Now Jesus had not yet come into the village, but was still in the place where Martha had met him. 31 When the Jews who were with her in the house, consoling her, saw Mary rise quickly and go out, they followed her, supposing that she was going to the tomb to weep there. 32 Now when Mary came to where Jesus was and saw him, she fell at his feet, saying to him, "Lord, if you had been here, my brother would not have died." 33 When Jesus saw her weeping, and the Jews who had come with her also weeping, he was deeply moved in his spirit and greatly troubled. 34 And he said, "Where have you laid him?" They said to him, "Lord, come and see." 35 Jesus wept. 36 So the Jews said, "See how he loved him!" 37 But some of them said, "Could not he who opened the eyes of the blind man also have kept this man from dying?"

38 Then Jesus, deeply moved again, came to the tomb. It was a cave, and
a stone lay against it. 39 Jesus said, "Take away the stone." Martha, the sister
of the dead man, said to him, "Lord, by this time there will be an odor, for he
has been dead four days." 40 Jesus said to her, "Did I not tell you that if you
believed you would see the glory of God?" 41 So they took away the stone. And
Jesus lifted up his eyes and said, "Father, I thank you that you have heard
me. 42 I knew that you always hear me, but I said this on account of the people
standing around, that they may believe that you sent me." 43 When he had said
these things, he cried out with a loud voice, "Lazarus, come out." 44 The man
who had died came out, his hands and feet bound with linen strips, and his
face wrapped with a cloth. Jesus said to them, "Unbind him, and let him go."

45 Many of the Jews therefore, who had come with Mary and had seen what
he did, believed in him, 46 but some of them went to the Pharisees and told
them what Jesus had done.

12:1 Six days before the Passover, Jesus therefore came to Bethany, where
Lazarus was, whom Jesus had raised from the dead. 2 So they gave a dinner
for him there. Martha served, and Lazarus was one of those reclining with
him at table. 3 Mary therefore took a pound of expensive ointment made from
pure nard, and anointed the feet of Jesus and wiped his feet with her hair.
The house was filled with the fragrance of the perfume. 4 But Judas Iscariot,
one of his disciples (he who was about to betray him), said, 5 "Why was this
ointment not sold for three hundred denarii and given to the poor?" 6 He said
this, not because he cared about the poor, but because he was a thief, and
having charge of the moneybag he used to help himself to what was put into
it. 7 Jesus said, "Leave her alone, so that she may keep it for the day of my
burial. 8 For the poor you always have with you, but you do not always have me."

NOTES

OBSERVE: WHAT DOES THE PASSAGE SAY?

Step 1: Setting and Summary

Key Characters and Locations

CHARACTERS:

LOCATIONS:

Summary of the Passage

What Stood Out to You or Piqued Your Curiosity?

Step 2: Key Words and Phrases

NOTES

INTERPRET: WHAT DOES THE PASSAGE MEAN?

Step 3: What Was Hard to Understand?

Questions

Insights from Cross-References, Other Translations, and the Context

Step 4: What Did You Learn about God?

Refer to the attributes of God in Tool 4 if needed.

What did you learn about God's view of women?

NOTES

APPLY: HOW WILL YOU APPLY THE PASSAGE?

Step 5: What Did You Learn about People?

Others

Yourself

Wrap Up: What Did You Discover in the Scriptures That Was Important to You?

8

THE WOMAN AT THE WELL AND THE WOMAN CAUGHT IN ADULTERY

John 4:1–29, 39; 8:1–11

THE WOMAN AT THE WELL AND THE WOMAN CAUGHT IN ADULTERY

Context for the Stories of the Woman at the Well and the Woman Caught in Adultery

Where Are We in the Story of the Bible?

Turn to Tool 1 in the Tool Kit and place an *X* after the incarnation and before the crucifixion, resurrection, and ascension. Pencil in the titles of these two women there.

During the beginning of his public ministry, Jesus traveled through towns and villages, preaching and proclaiming the good news of the kingdom of God. The twelve disciples traveled with him, along with others. He attracted large crowds and created quite a stir wherever he went. He spoke in parables, cast out demons, healed the sick, forgave sins, calmed storms, and taught with authority. He not only preached to crowds; he also spoke with individuals, giving them his full attention.

Who Is the Woman at the Well?

The woman at the well lived in Samaria. The Samaritan people were avoided and looked down upon by the Jewish people of Galilee and Judea (Judea is "Judah" in Greek). This social animosity was rooted in Old Testament history. When the nation of Israel was divided into two kingdoms after Solomon's reign—Israel to the north and Judah to the south—many of the Jews in the "new" northern Israel intermarried with the pagan cultures around them. The Samaritan people resulted from the intermarrying.

It was considered unfit for Jesus, a Jewish rabbi, to ask for a drink from a Samaritan, and it was frowned upon for an unmarried, Jewish man to speak to a woman alone. This did not stop Jesus. He traveled to Samaria with purpose—to speak to the woman at the well. The woman at the well was scorned not only by Jews but most likely by her own people as well, indicated by the fact that she chose to go to the well at the hottest, and least populated, part of the day.

Who Is the Woman Caught in Adultery?

The Scriptures do not give details about this woman. She was used as a pawn by the Pharisees to attempt to trap Jesus. They were desperate for a reason to arrest him.

Read the passages to see their stories unfold.

John 4:1–29, 39; 8:1–11

4:1 Now when Jesus learned that the Pharisees had heard that Jesus was
making and baptizing more disciples than John 2 (although Jesus himself
did not baptize, but only his disciples), 3 he left Judea and departed again
for Galilee. 4 And he had to pass through Samaria. 5 So he came to a town of
Samaria called Sychar, near the field that Jacob had given to his son Joseph.
6 Jacob's well was there; so Jesus, wearied as he was from his journey, was
sitting beside the well. It was about the sixth hour.

7 A woman from Samaria came to draw water. Jesus said to her, "Give me
a drink." 8 (For his disciples had gone away into the city to buy food.) 9 The
Samaritan woman said to him, "How is it that you, a Jew, ask for a drink from
me, a woman of Samaria?" (For Jews have no dealings with Samaritans.)
10 Jesus answered her, "If you knew the gift of God, and who it is that is saying to you, 'Give me a drink,' you would have asked him, and he would have
given you living water." 11 The woman said to him, "Sir, you have nothing to
draw water with, and the well is deep. Where do you get that living water?
12 Are you greater than our father Jacob? He gave us the well and drank from
it himself, as did his sons and his livestock." 13 Jesus said to her, "Everyone
who drinks of this water will be thirsty again, 14 but whoever drinks of the
water that I will give him will never be thirsty again. The water that I will
give him will become in him a spring of water welling up to eternal life."
15 The woman said to him, "Sir, give me this water, so that I will not be thirsty
or have to come here to draw water."

16 Jesus said to her, "Go, call your husband, and come here." 17 The woman answered him, "I have no husband." Jesus said to her, "You are right in saying, 'I have no husband'; 18 for you have had five husbands, and the one you now have is not your husband. What you have said is true." 19 The woman said to him, "Sir, I perceive that you are a prophet. 20 Our fathers worshiped on this mountain, but you say that in Jerusalem is the place where people ought to worship." 21 Jesus said to her, "Woman, believe me, the hour is coming when neither on this mountain nor in Jerusalem will you worship the Father. 22 You worship what you do not know; we worship what we know, for salvation is from the Jews. 23 But the hour is coming, and is now here, when the true worshipers will worship the Father in spirit and truth, for the Father is seeking such people to worship him. 24 God is spirit, and those who worship him must worship in spirit and truth." 25 The woman said to him, "I know that Messiah is coming (he who is called Christ). When he comes, he will tell us all things." 26 Jesus said to her, "I who speak to you am he."

27 Just then his disciples came back. They marveled that he was talking with a woman, but no one said, "What do you seek?" or, "Why are you talking with her?" 28 So the woman left her water jar and went away into town and said to the people, 29 "Come, see a man who told me all that I ever did. Can this be the Christ?" . . .

39 Many Samaritans from that town believed in him because of the woman's testimony, "He told me all that I ever did."

8:1 Jesus went to the Mount of Olives. 2 Early in the morning he came again to the temple. All the people came to him, and he sat down and taught them. 3 The scribes and the Pharisees brought a woman who had been caught in adultery, and placing her in the midst 4 they said to him, "Teacher, this woman has been caught in the act of adultery. 5 Now in the Law, Moses commanded us to stone such women. So what do you say?" 6 This they said to test him,

that they might have some charge to bring against him. Jesus bent down
and wrote with his finger on the ground. [7] And as they continued to ask him,
he stood up and said to them, "Let him who is without sin among you be the
first to throw a stone at her." [8] And once more he bent down and wrote on the
ground. [9] But when they heard it, they went away one by one, beginning with
the older ones, and Jesus was left alone with the woman standing before
him. [10] Jesus stood up and said to her, "Woman, where are they? Has no one
condemned you?" [11] She said, "No one, Lord." And Jesus said, "Neither do
I condemn you; go, and from now on sin no more."

NOTES

OBSERVE: WHAT DOES THE PASSAGE SAY?

Step 1: Setting and Summary

Key Characters and Locations

CHARACTERS:

LOCATIONS:

Summary of the Passage

What Stood Out to You or Piqued Your Curiosity?

Step 2: Key Words and Phrases

NOTES

INTERPRET: WHAT DOES THE PASSAGE MEAN?

Step 3: What Was Hard to Understand?

Questions

Insights from Cross-References, Other Translations, and the Context

Step 4: What Did You Learn about God?

Refer to the attributes of God in Tool 4 if needed.

What did you learn about God's view of women?

NOTES

APPLY: HOW WILL YOU APPLY THE PASSAGE?

Step 5: What Did You Learn about People?

Others

Yourself

Wrap Up: What Did You Discover in the Scriptures That Was Important to You?

MEET ME IN THE BIBLE TOOL KIT

Tool 1

BIBLE TIMELINE

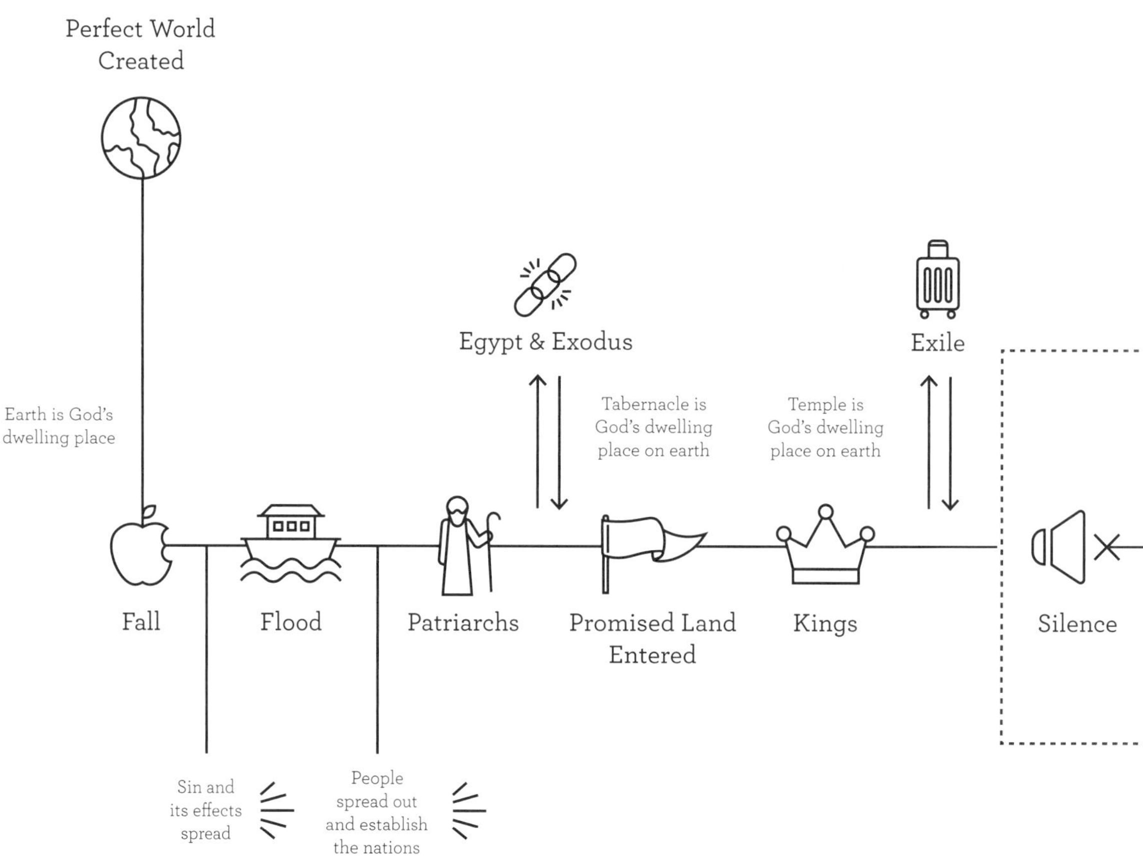

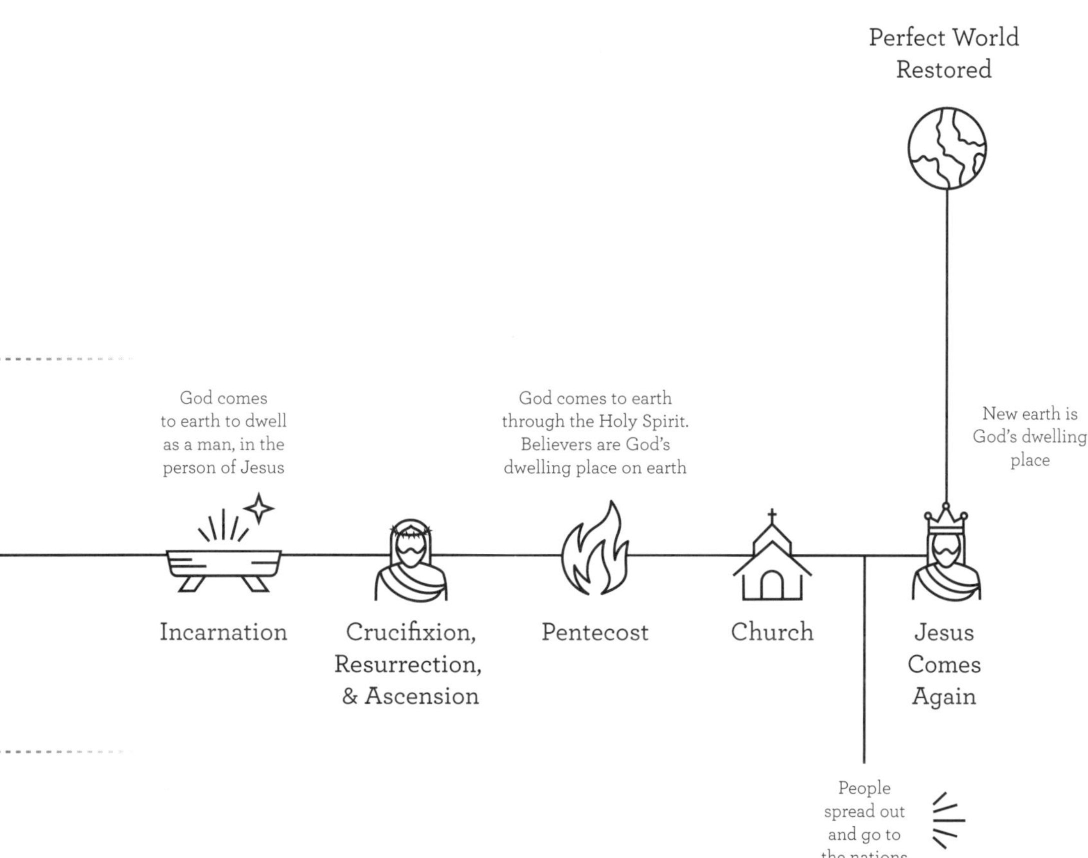
Perfect World
Restored
God comes
to earth to dwell
as a man, in the
person of Jesus
God comes to earth
through the Holy Spirit.
Believers are God's
dwelling place on earth
New earth is
God's dwelling
place
Incarnation
Crucifixion,
Resurrection,
& Ascension
Pentecost
Church
Jesus
Comes
Again
People
spread out
and go to
the nations

Tool 2

MAPS OF THE ANCIENT NEAR EAST

The World of the Patriarchs

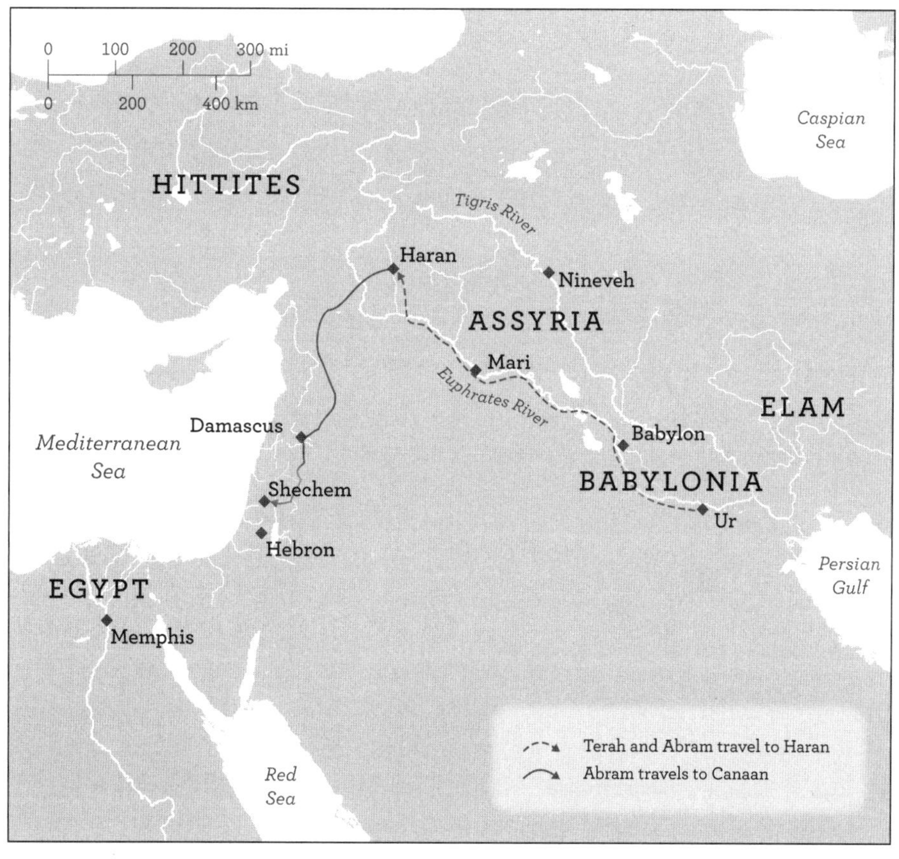

The Tribal Allotments of Israel

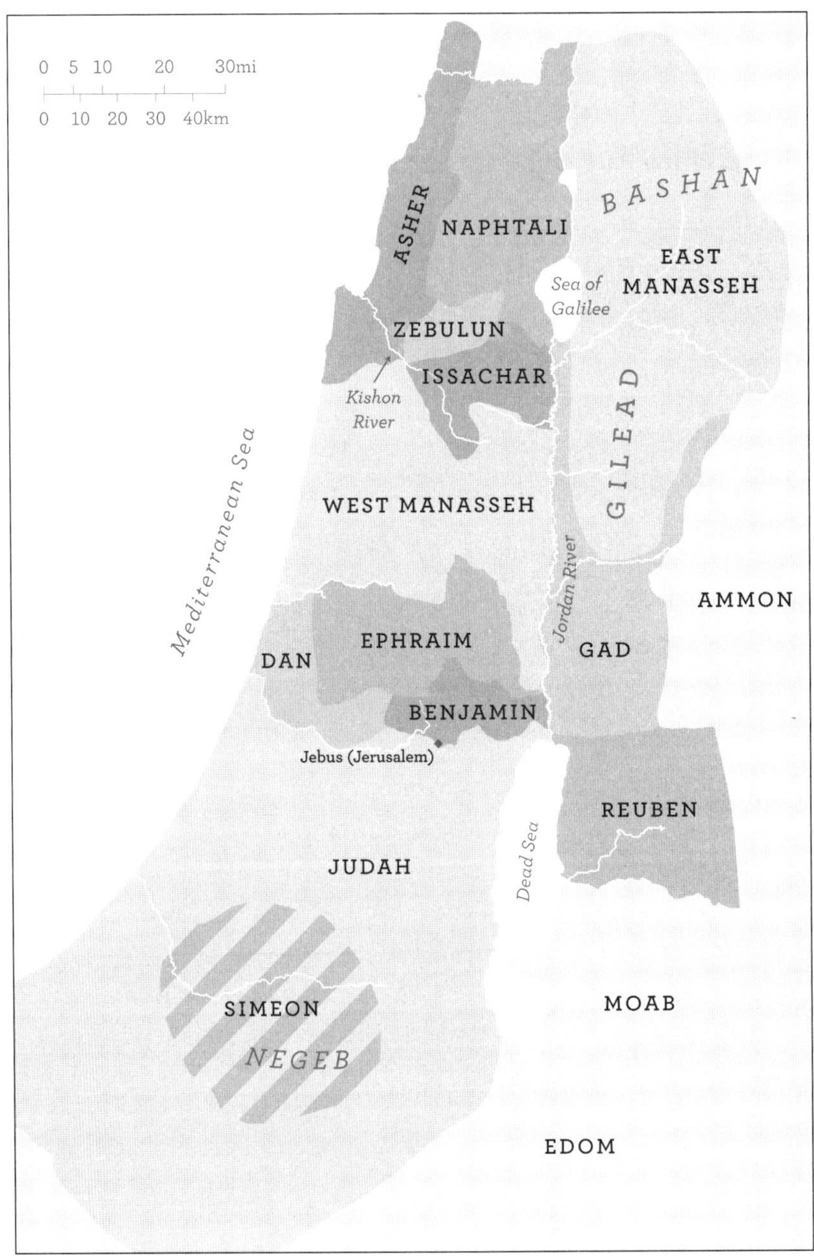

Palestine under Roman Rule

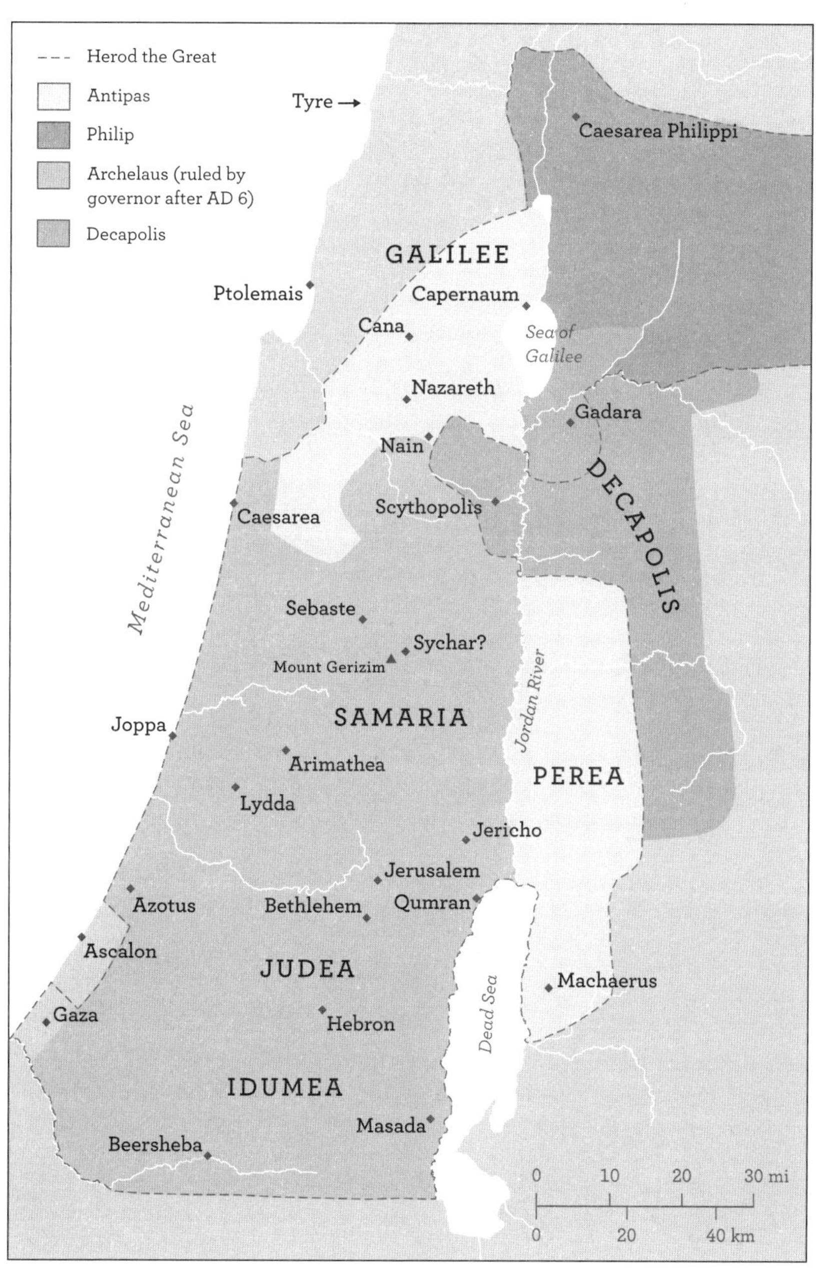

Tool 3

BIBLE GENRES

Knowing the literary style of the book of the Bible you are studying is key to correct interpretation. Just as you would approach the poems of Wordsworth differently than you would approach a history book about World War II, there are nuances to different literary styles in the Bible that must be kept in mind while interpreting and applying the Scriptures. Use this resource to identify the literary style of the book you are studying. Note that several books can be classified in more than one genre.

Genres	Books of the Bible
Apocalyptic. Visionary writings that address future judgment and salvation. Often written using symbolic language.	Daniel, Revelation
Epistle. Letters to Christians in the early church that contain doctrines of the Christian faith and instructions for Christlike living.	Romans, 1–2 Corinthians, Galatians, Ephesians, Philippians, Colossians, 1–2 Thessalonians, 1–2 Timothy, Titus, Philemon, Hebrews, James, 1–2 Peter, 1–3 John, Jude
Gospel. Historical narratives that give testimony to the genealogy, birth, life, death, resurrection, and teachings of Jesus Christ. Each Gospel is written by a different author from a different perspective and with a different emphasis.	Matthew, Mark, Luke, John

Genres	Books of the Bible
Historical Narrative. Narrations of the factual history of Israel and the early church. Historical narratives are recordings of what happened, not necessarily what should have happened had people obeyed God's commands.	Genesis, Exodus, Leviticus, Numbers, Deuteronomy, Joshua, Judges, Ruth, 1–2 Samuel, 1–2 Kings, 1–2 Chronicles, Ezra, Nehemiah, Esther, Jonah, Acts
Poetry. Expressions of joy, thanksgiving, celebration, disappointment, anxiety, and lament in poetic forms.	Psalms, Song of Solomon, Lamentations
Prophecy. God's message to his people spoken through prophets, calling God's people to repentance from sin, warning them of judgment, and revealing events yet to come.	Isaiah, Jeremiah, Ezekiel, Daniel, Hosea, Joel, Amos, Obadiah, Jonah, Micah, Nahum, Habakkuk, Zephaniah, Haggai, Zechariah, Malachi
Wisdom Literature. Writings that address life's basic questions about what it means to live faithful, God-centered lives in both big crises and everyday circumstances.	Job, some Psalms, Proverbs, Ecclesiastes

Tool 4

ATTRIBUTES OF GOD

Attentive. God hears and responds to the needs of his children.

Compassionate. God cares for his children and acts on their behalf.

Creator. God made everything. He is uncreated.

Deliverer. God rescues and saves his children.

Eternal. God is not limited by and exists outside of time.

Faithful. God always keeps his promises.

Generous. God gives what is best and beyond what is deserved.

Glorious. God displays his greatness and worth.

Good. God is what is best and gives what is best.

Holy. God is perfect, pure, and without sin.

Immutable/Unchanging. God never changes. He is the same yesterday, today, and tomorrow.

Incomprehensible. God is beyond our understanding. We can comprehend him in part but not in whole.

Infinite. God has no limits in his person or on his power.

Jealous. God will not share his glory with another. All glory rightfully belongs to him.

Just. God is fair in all his actions and judgments. He cannot overpunish or underpunish.

Loving. God feels and displays infinite, unconditional affection toward his children. His love for them does not depend on their worth, their response, or their merit.

Merciful. God does not give his children the punishment they deserve.

Omnipotent/Almighty. God holds all power. Nothing is too hard for God. What he wills he can accomplish.

Omnipresent. God is fully present everywhere.

Omniscient. God knows everything past, present, and future, all potential and real outcomes, all things micro and macro.

Patient/Long-Suffering. God is untiring and bears with his children.

Provider. God meets the needs of his children.

Refuge. God is a place of safety and protection for his children.

Righteous. God is always good and right.

Self-Existent. God depends on nothing and no one to give him life or existence.

Sovereign. God does everything according to his plan and pleasure. He controls all things.

Transcendent. God is not like humans. He is infinitely higher in being and action.

Truthful. Whatever God speaks or does is truth and reality.

Wise. God knows what is best and acts accordingly. He cannot choose wrongly.

Worthy. God deserves all glory and honor and praise.

Wrathful. God hates all unrighteousness.

Tool 5

BOOKMARK CONTENT

Begin by asking God to reveal himself as you read the Scriptures. Enjoy him and have fun learning and discovering!

Observe: What Does the Passage Say?

Step 1. Setting and Summary

- Read the passage, noting key characters and locations.
- Write a brief summary of the passage (about three to five sentences).
- Record what stood out to you or piqued your curiosity.

Step 2. Key Words and Phrases

- Read the passage, marking the words/phrases that are repeated or emphasized.
- Why do you think the author repeats these words? Look back at the context to help you with your answer (e.g., Who wrote it and to whom was it written?). Write down your insights.
- Are there words for which you need a better understanding (e.g., *propitiation, atonement*)? Use a dictionary or thesaurus to gain insight and note what you discover.
- Read the verses with key words/phrases in two other Bible translations. Jot down what you learn.
- Enjoy God. Talk to him and listen.

Interpret: What Does the Passage Mean?

Step 3. What Was Hard to Understand?

- Read the passage, writing down the questions that surface for you.

- Record insights you gain from the following:
    - Looking up cross-references for verses that are hard to understand.
    - Reading the passage in two other Bible translations.
    - Looking back at the context (e.g., Who wrote it and to whom was it written and when?).

Step 4. What Did You Learn about God?

- What attribute of God stood out to you in this passage?
- How does this attribute of God encourage you to anchor your hope in him? Record your discoveries.
- Enjoy God. Talk to him and listen.

Apply: How Will You Apply the Passage?

Step 5. What Did You Learn about People?

OTHERS

- What did you learn about people in this passage? How does this passage promote a love for others? Write down your thoughts.
- What did you learn that you can share with others (a friend, coworker, family member)? Pray for meaningful conversations this week.

YOURSELF

- Is there a command to obey? An example to follow? A sin to confess? A warning to heed? An encouragement to receive? Record your insights.
- What action step will you take? How will next week be different because you chose to apply what you discovered?
- Enjoy God. Talk to him and listen.

Tool 6

PRAYER PAGES

PRAYER PAGE

PRAYER PAGE

PRAYER PAGE

PRAYER PAGE

PRAYER PAGE

PRAYER PAGE

PRAYER PAGE

Tool 7

QUESTIONS FOR FURTHER THOUGHT AND DISCUSSION

These questions were written to help you think deeply about the text. Additional historical context is also given. Many questions do not have one right answer and are meant to encourage further thought and robust discussion. The bounce questions are intended to jumpstart discussion and provide an easy transition to the content.

Discussion leaders may use as many or as few questions as they'd like. The prompts on your bookmark also make good points of discussion.

Getting Started in the Stories of Women

1. Why do you want to study stories of women in the Bible?
2. As you answered the context questions found in "Getting Started in Stories of Women," what new insight did you gain?
3. What piqued your curiosity?
4. Complete the sentence: At the end of this study, I hope to ____________.

Sarah and Hagar (Genesis 11:29–12:3; 16:1–16; 18:10–15; 21:1–21)

- Bounce question: Have you ever waited a long time for something that really mattered to you? If yes, describe.

1. How would you describe Abraham and Sarah's relationship?
2. What do you think Hagar was feeling and thinking when Sarah (formerly named Sarai) offered her to Abraham to fulfill God's promise of offspring? Do you think Hagar had a choice?

3. How would you describe Sarah's actions in these chapters? How about Abraham's? Can you think of a time when you attempted to "help" God keep his promise? How did it go?
4. The Scriptures tell us that God *found* Hagar in the wilderness. What does this tell us about God? Look back at the helpful hint given on page 16 as you consider how God demonstrated love for Hagar.
5. In light of Genesis 16, 18, and 21, how would you describe Sarah's relationship with God? How about Hagar's?
6. Both Sarah and Hagar submitted to God in difficult ways. In what way(s) did Sarah yield to God's plan rather than pursuing her own? How about Hagar? What can we learn from them?
7. In what way(s) did God demonstrate his goodness to Abraham? To Sarah? To Hagar? Did God have a favorite?
8. Did you relate to one of the key characters (Abraham, Sarah, Hagar) of the text? If yes, how so?

Leah and Rachel (Genesis 29:1–35; 30:1–24; and 49:28–33)

- Bounce question: Describe a moment of sibling rivalry from your childhood. Why do you think sibling rivalry exists to some degree in every family?

1. What do you think Leah was feeling as she dressed for her wedding? Do you think Leah had a choice? How do you think Rachel felt on what was supposed to be her wedding day?
2. Why do you think Laban deceived Jacob in this way? What did Laban gain? Look back at Genesis 24:29–31, when Laban met Abraham's servant, for insight.
3. What choice did Jacob have to make after he woke up next to Leah? Do you think God was pleased with his choice? Use Scripture to back up your answer. How did his choice affect Leah? Rachel?

4. What did you learn about Leah through the names of her sons? What is the implication of Leah being the mother of Judah (Matt. 1:1–6)?
5. Leah and Rachel competed for the love of one man. What was their strategy for securing favor? Look back at the helpful hint on page 28 as you consider.
6. In what way(s) did God demonstrate his goodness to Leah? To Rachel? To Jacob? Did God have a favorite?
7. Did you relate to one of the key characters (Jacob, Leah, Rachel, Laban) in the text? If yes, how so?

Women in Exodus (Exodus 1:1–22; 2:1–10)

- Bounce question: Have you lived in another culture for an extended time? What were the challenges?

1. Did the midwives do wrong when they deceived Pharaoh about the Hebrew women? Did it surprise you that God blessed them? Why or why not?
2. How will a healthy fear of God help you act courageously in your culture?
3. What do you think Jochebed was feeling when she made the basket for her baby?
4. How did Jochebed demonstrate courage? How did Miriam? Pharaoh's daughter?
5. Pharaoh's daughter named the baby "Moses," which sounds like the Hebrew verb that means "to draw out." Moses was later *drawn out* of the Egyptian palace, to *draw out* his people from Egypt. In what way(s) is God compelling you to be *drawn out* from the world in obedience to him?
6. In what ways does God demonstrate his goodness to the midwives? To Jochebed? To Miriam? (Look up Exodus 15:19–21 for a peek into Miriam's future role.) To Pharaoh's daughter?

7. Who did Pharaoh discount as a threat to his power (Ex. 1:22)? Have fun discussing the irony of this.

8. Moses was inspired by the Holy Spirit to record these stories of brave women in Exodus who helped deliver Israel's deliverer. What does this communicate about God's view of women?

Deborah and Jael (Judges 2:11–23; 4:1–24; 5:1–9, 19–31)

- Bounce question: Have you known women who faced danger in answering God's call to leadership? If yes, please describe.

1. What provoked the Lord to anger in Judges 2? What were the consequences for the Israelites?

2. What do we know about Deborah from these passages?

3. What do you learn about Jael? (Review Judg. 5:24–27.) What hint from the text do you see that Jael was accustomed to driving tent pegs into the ground?

4. What do you think about Judges 2:16; 4:4; and 4:8–9? Why do you think God chose women to lead and battle for Israel?

5. What kind of man was Sisera? What did he include in his spoils of war? (See Judg. 5:30.) What does "a womb or two for every man" mean? How does this add to your understanding of praise for Jael's actions?

6. What do you learn about God's view of women from these passages?

Elizabeth and Mary (Luke 1:1–66)

- Bounce question: Do you have a close relationship with a cousin? What is special about this relationship?

1. Both Zechariah and Mary asked Gabriel a question. Why do you think Gabriel responded differently to each?

2. Did you learn something new about Elizabeth or Mary? If yes, what?

3. What did Elizabeth's and Mary's pregnancies have in common? In what ways do you think Elizabeth's pregnancy was challenging? How about Mary's?

4. Why do you think Mary went with haste to Elizabeth's house? How would you describe the relationship between Mary and Elizabeth?

5. Mary's song of praise includes many phrases from the Old Testament psalms and prophets. What does this imply about Mary?

6. In Luke 1:51, Mary said of the Lord, "He has scattered the proud in the thoughts of their hearts." Can you think of another passsage in the Bible that describes God purposefully scattering the proud?

7. Read Genesis 3:15. Google the painting *Mary Consoles Eve* by Grace Remington and discuss.

8. How did God demonstrate his goodness to Zechariah? To Elizabeth? To Mary? To the Jews?

Anna and Tabitha (Luke 2:22–38; Acts 9:36–43)

- Bounce question: Describe an older woman who has influenced you or challenged you to image God in a new way.

1. The Scriptures tell us that Anna was from the tribe of Asher. You can see where his tribe settled on the map titled "The Tribal Allotments of Israel" in Tool 2 of the Tool Kit. In the story of Jacob, Leah, and Rachel, we learn that Asher was not the son of Jacob's favorite wife, Rachel. He was not the son of the hated wife, Leah. He was the youngest son of Leah's servant (Gen. 30:9–13). Asher was considered least among the twelve tribes of Israel. Why do you think Luke included this detail about Anna?

2. Life did not turn out like Anna thought it would. About how many years did Anna spend as a widow? How did she choose to spend her time?

3. Remember that no prophet had spoken for four hundred years before Jesus was born. What title do the Scriptures give Anna in Luke 2:36? What do you think she prophesied about? (See Luke 2:38.)
4. Look at Acts 9:36 and correct the wrong word as it appears here: "Now there was in Joppa a woman named Tabitha, which, translated, means Dorcas." Considering how the culture viewed women at the time, why is this word significant?
5. What do you read, or not read, in Acts 9:36–43 that implies Tabitha was a single woman?
6. Read Deuteronomy 10:17–18; 14:29 and James 1:27. Why do you think the care of widows is so important to God? In what particular way did Tabitha join God in his ministry for widows?
7. Did you relate to Anna or Tabitha? If yes, how so?
8. How did God demonstrate his goodness to Anna? To Tabitha? To the widows Tabitha served?

Martha and Mary (Luke 10:38–42; John 11:1–46; 12:1–8)

- Bounce Question: Do you have a sibling who interprets life through a different lens from you? If yes, please describe.

1. Remember from the helpful hint on page 86 that Jewish custom highly regarded hospitality, and hosting was a cultural expectation. Martha was right to serve as a hostess for Jesus and those who were with him. The word *distracted* in the original language means to be cumbered, burdened, or dragged away. With all this in mind, what went wrong in this scenario?
2. In Luke 10:42, what do you think is the "one thing [that] is necessary"?
3. Can you think of any cultural expectations that burden you or even drag you away from the one thing that is necessary? If yes, what steps will you take to prevent this?

4. The words in John 11:5–6 are so surprising. Why do you think Jesus waited two days before going to Lazarus, Martha, and Mary?

5. After Lazarus's death, Martha and Mary would have been following the Jewish custom of "sitting shiva," gathering in mourning for seven days with other family members and friends (John 11:19). According to John 11:20, was Martha cumbered by cultural expectations and customs in this scenario?

6. The scene in John 12:1–8 took place the week before Jesus was arrested. Many Bible scholars believe that Mary's alabaster jar of costly and highly fragrant nard was her entire inheritance. If this is so, how does this add to the meaning of her gift?

7. How did Jesus demonstrate his love for Martha? For Mary? Did he have a favorite?

The Woman at the Well and the Woman Caught in Adultery (John 4:1–29, 39; 8:1–11)

- Bounce Question: Can you think of a time when God used someone else's testimony to incite change in you?

1. Look back at page 98 under "Who Is the Woman at the Well?" for a reminder about the tension between Jews and Samaritans. When traveling between Judea and Galilee, it was customary for Jewish religious leaders to take another road around Samaria to avoid contact with Samaritans. How might this historical context add meaning to John 4:4? In other words, why did Jesus have to pass through Samaria?

2. The sixth hour was noon. Why was this an unusual time for a woman to be at the well drawing water? What does this tell us about her?

3. What do you think Jesus meant when he said he could give her living water? What do you think she was thirsty for?

4. Who did the woman go toward, according to John 4:28? Who do you think she had been avoiding by drawing water at noon? Can

you think of a time you were willing to move toward those you had avoided after an encounter with Jesus?

5. What was the motive of the scribes and Pharisees for bringing in the woman caught in adultery, recorded in John 8?
6. What do you learn about God's view of women from these passages?
7. What did you learn from this study that you hope never to forget?

NOTES

1. My favorite tool is Merriam-Webster's Collegiate Dictionary, 11th ed. (Springfield, MA: Merriam-Webster, 2003), continually updated at https://www.merriam-webster.com.
2. I demonstrate how to use Bible Gateway (https://www.biblegateway.com/) to cross-reference in my introductory video: https://www.colleensearcy.com/.
3. Bible Gateway (https://www.biblegateway.com/) also includes footnotes.
4. I've found Tim Challies's article helpful: "Best Commentaries on Each Book of the Bible," Challies website, accessed April 29, 2024, https://challies.com/.
5. For further study on Bible genres, a helpful resource is Gordon D. Fee and Douglas Stuart, *How to Read the Bible for All Its Worth* (Grand Rapids, MI: Zondervan, 2014).
6. Merriam-Webster, s.v. "contempt," accessed July 20, 2024, https://www.merriam-webster.com/.

Meet Me in the Bible

For more information, visit **crossway.org**.